AF327187

A PAINTER AND HIS WIFE

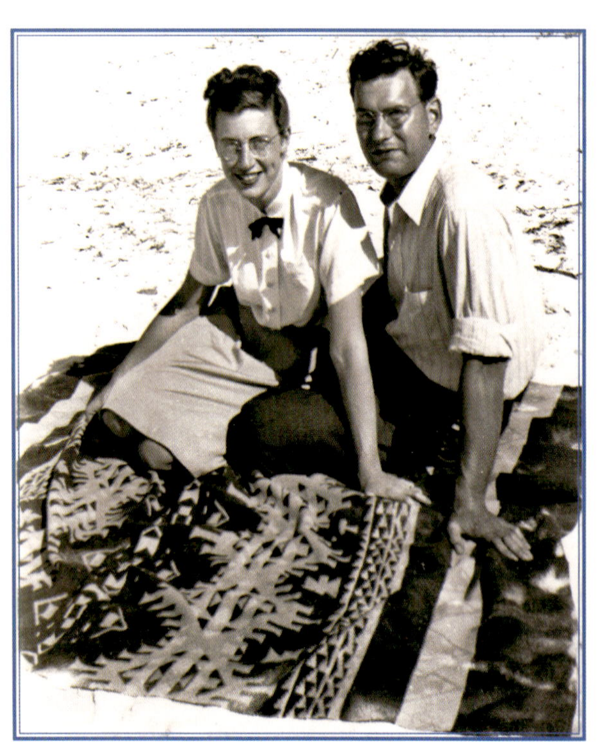

A PAINTER AND HIS WIFE

A MEMOIR

ELDEN ROWLAND · PAINTER
KATHERINE ROWLAND · WIFE

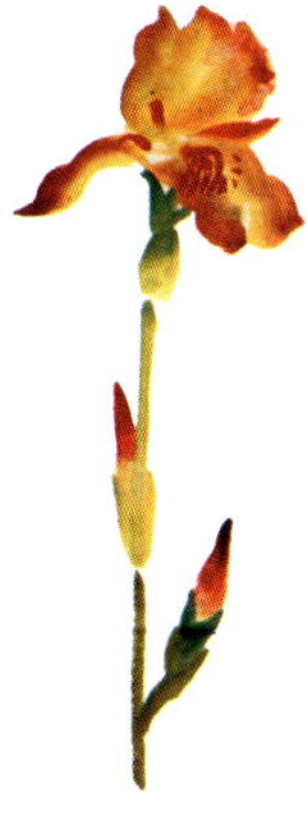

BY
KATHERINE LOLLAR ROWLAND

ORANGE FRAZER PRESS
WILMINGTON, OHIO

Copyright 2006 Katherine Lollar Rowland

Published by Orange Frazer Press.

No part of this publication may be reproduced or transmitted in any form or by any means, electronic or mechanical, including any information storage and retrieval systems without permission from the author and publisher, except by reviewers who wish to quote briefly.

Additional copies may be ordered
KATHERINE L. ROWLAND
4033 BLUEBIRD COURT
LEBANON, OHIO 45036
513-932-4975
kathworld@aol.com
website: katherinelollarrowland.com

Designed by Chad DeBoard

Printed in China

Library of Congress Control Number: 2006921942

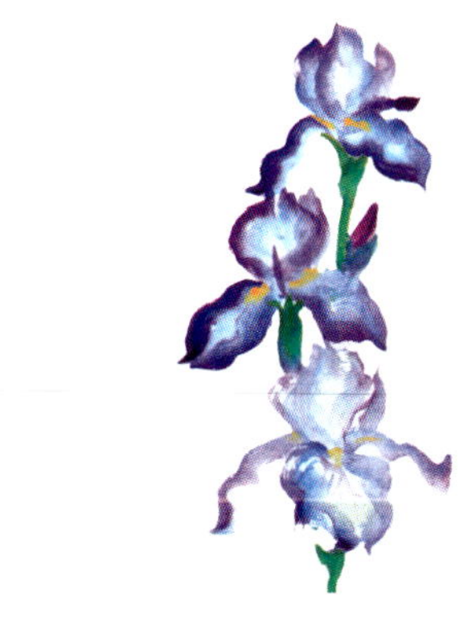

TO ELDEN
AND ALL THE OTHERS
WHO MADE OUR LIFE MEMORABLE

PREFACE

On V-J Day, August 15, 1945, with the closing gun of World War II, my husband, Elden, walked out of a machine shop where he had been helping to make tank parts for the Russians—never to go back again.

We bought a house trailer, and started out to pursue his dream of becoming a fine artist. Prior to the War Elden had been a commercial artist, doing minute detailed drawings for the Yellow Pages of the phone book. I, trained as a stenographer and secretary, had worked in various business offices. We had grown up less than thirty miles from each other in Southwest Ohio, but from vastly different backgrounds.

Elden was a city boy from Norwood, a suburb of Cincinnati. I grew up on the Lollar farm, in what was then almost entirely rural Warren County. Elden, who always liked to draw and do things with his hands, took children's classes at the Cincinnati Art Museum and developed an early interest in Oriental things. When he dropped out of high school he had already learned much about Eastern art, culture, philosophy, and religion. I went to The Ridge, the one-room school near my home, graduated from Lebanon High School, and attended business school in Cincinnati.

Fate brought us together when my first job was at an insurance office, where Marjory, Elden's sister, also worked.

A Painter and His Wife is the story of our full and varied life after we left Ohio; and of the many people whose lives enriched ours along the way, especially three couples: Helen Sawyer and Jerry Farnsworth; Eleanor Treacy and Eric Hodgins; and Dorothy Sherman and Hilton Leech.

Integrating reproductions into the text, it traces Elden's development as an artist: his painting, his teaching and his philosophy. It is not a history, as such, but all quotations and references have been taken from primary source material, such as newspapers, catalogs and correspondence. It is also the story of the sometimes surprising ways that opened up for me to make my own contribution in the world of art and letters.

On September 24, 1945—my 27th birthday—Elden and I began our adventure following his dream of becoming an artist. We had accomplished much in the six weeks between the exhilarating release that came with V-J Day on August 15, and our departure from 4000 St. Johns Terrace, Deer Park, Cincinnati, Ohio.

We evolved a plan. We would buy a house trailer and travel for three years while he learned to paint. Vaguely, we thought that at the end of that time we would return to live again in southwest Ohio. However, we never did. That dream, like a hot-air balloon released from its tether, simply took off and soared in its own uncharted path for the rest of our lives.

Our neighbors, Harold and Nolia Werner, agreed to rent the home we had so proudly purchased a couple of years before because it had a spare bedroom for Elden to use to draw and paint. We bought a used 14-foot house trailer, although we soon replaced it with a newer, 16-foot, Covered Wagon. That was an important part of preparing us for our new life because, in remodeling it, Elden learned to work with wood. Dr. Werner, although an executive with a pharmaceutical company, was an expert carpenter and instructed Elden as they worked together in the remodeling.

Even during the war years, Elden and his friends, Rosemary and Ed Clapper, had eked out enough gas coupons to take short painting excursions. "Bean Blossom, Indiana," was the first watercolor he did on location. His entry in his little black book records it as "#1, painted August 1943, sold to Dot Lollar." This was a fortunate thing because Dot Lollar was my brother Bob's wife and the painting, with others of his early works, has remained in the family and available to be photographed for this book.

"Spring Mill," #2, watercolor, was shown in the 1945 Juried Exhibition of Cincinnati Artists at the Museum in Eden Park. Spring Mill State Park, one of Indiana's excellent resorts, was near enough to our home for wartime vacations. "Katherine Reading," a pastel, #7 in the list, was my first posing experience, a forerunner of many to come.

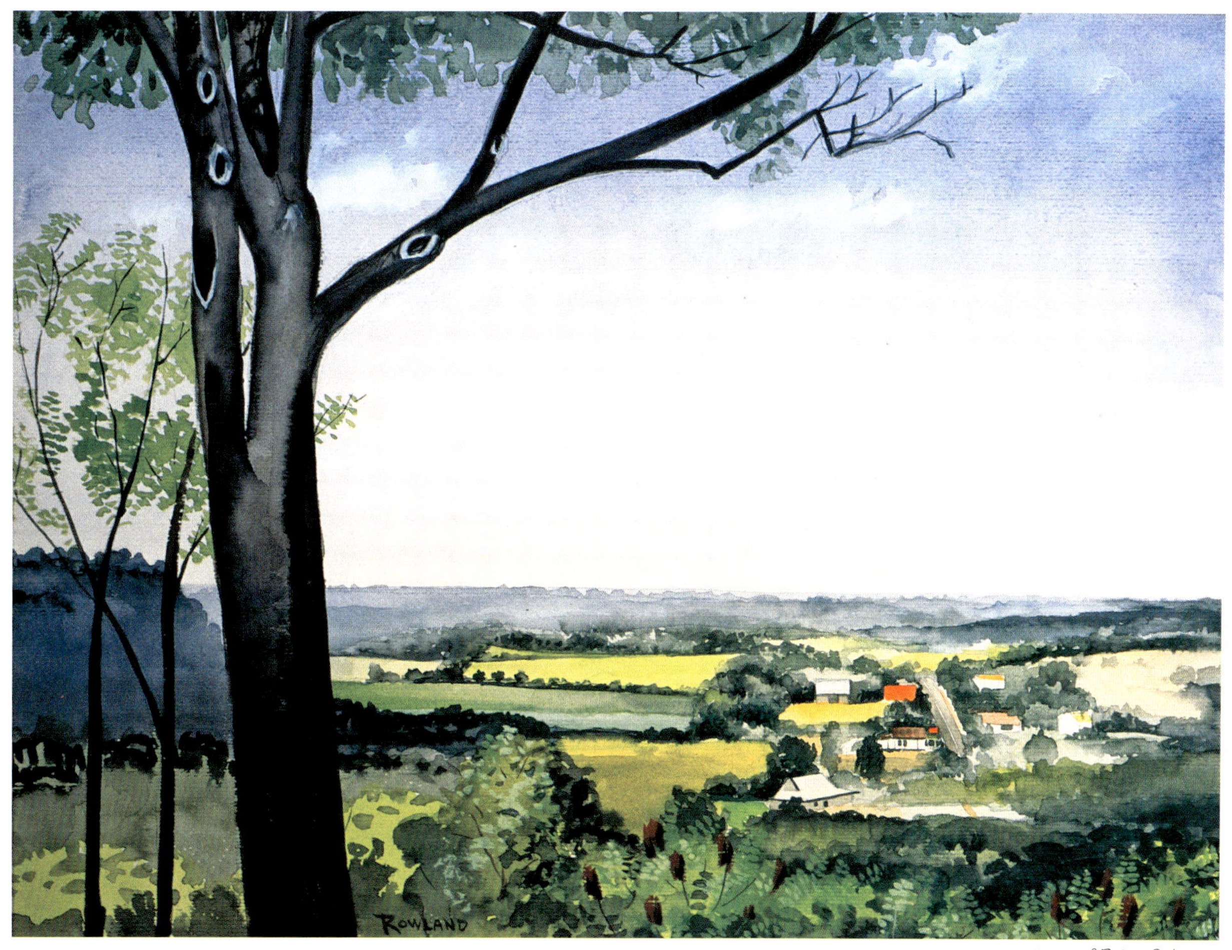

courtesy of Brian Schwarz

Bean Blossom, Indiana
watercolor 1943

"The Roosa Place and the Little Miami River Hills" was the last painting Elden did before we packed all our belongings in the trailer and left Ohio. The Roosa Place, a part of the Lollar Farm, was so-named because of the notorious axe murders committed there in 1864. In 1945, because Elden was the only one immune to the all-encompassing poison ivy, he had taken one last day to clear out fencerows. In the 1970s, after new Highways I 71 and OH 48 took the corner of the farm, this old homestead with its leaning silo became the site of Fujitech, a Japanese firm making elevators and escalators and its test tower is visible for miles around.

Because our families were reluctant to have us go off on such a "wild" adventure, I agreed to write them every day. These Daily Letters, which Marjory Nash, Elden's sister, kept for us, became a journal of our trailer travels and beyond.

As Elden and I worked our way gradually southward that glorious fall of 1945, we found many sights and sounds and smells to excite our Midwestern sensibilities: tobacco fields and barns in Kentucky, Grand Ole Opry musicians in Tennessee, iron mines and sorghum mills in Alabama. The Daily Letters show no signs of stress. There were mentions of friendly people, baking cookies, walks in the moonlight, reading borrowed books and going to movies.

The first money earned came in Horse Cave, Kentucky, when Elden received $20 for painting the portrait of the little red-headed son and daughter of the owners of the trailer park, and I collected $1.50 for altering the little girl's snow suit.

Our first major stop was at Montgomery, Alabama. There Elden discovered a white-pillared Southern mansion filled with military couples waiting to be discharged from service. We knew one Army wife as "The Tampa Queen" because her husband had given that name to his bomber in her honor.

I got a job working for Syd Jacobs who had come down from New York to set up a temporary office in The Temple for the Jewish Federations and Welfare Funds. We were to see him later in New Orleans.

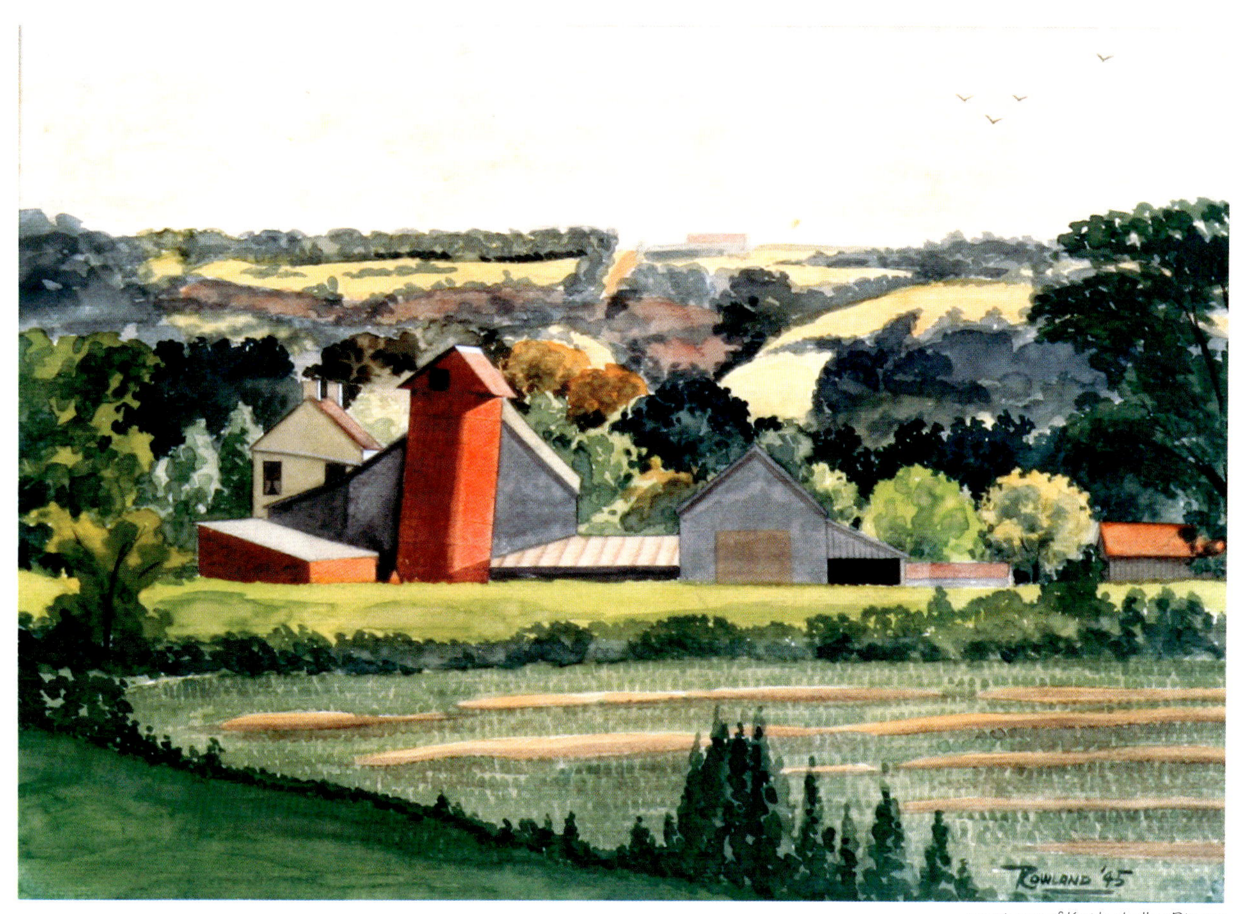

courtesy of Kathy Lollar Divens

THE ROOSA PLACE AND
LITTLE MIAMI RIVER HILLS
watercolor 1945

From Montgomery we continued south to Mobile Bay where Elden, who liked to carve model boats, was thrilled to see two old sailing vessels lying just where they had been left when they made their last trips hauling masts for sailing vessels from the live oak forests endemic to The South. A day's drive west across the Gulf Coast, at that time a long vista of ante-bellum estates and small-town docks before its splendor was dimmed by hurricanes and development, took us through the marshes of Louisiana to New Orleans.

New Orleans—long-anticipated, and just as colorful as we had expected! We snugged our trailer into a neat surround of long, serrated, green leaves, which we thought were palms. The next morning we awoke to find that the lush green growth was not palms but bananas, including pendulous wine-red blossoms and half-formed fruit, all dripping with three-inch icicles.

It warmed up and we soon found our way to the French Quarter—the fabulous Vieux Carre! Every place Elden looked there were scenes to paint and artists painting them. We met Alberta Kinsey, beloved for her pictures of magnolias and courtyards, who immediately took us to her heart when she learned I was from Lebanon, Ohio, where she had taught at the Normal University.

We became friends with John and LuNeal McReavy, and their small son Peter. John was a writer on disability pay from a war injury. Elden and he set up a barter system involving his Army officer's shirts so he could become a collector of Rowland paintings. John loved to talk, and like the shirts, was a part of our lives for many years to come.

Elden made himself at home in the French Quarter, finding quiet corners in little courtyards to paint when the lively streets scenes, as picturesque as they were, became too hectic. I went to work, part time, for my employer from Montgomery, Mr. Jacobs, who had come to New Orleans to set up a permanent office. AND—we explored the city, starting with French Quarter restaurants!

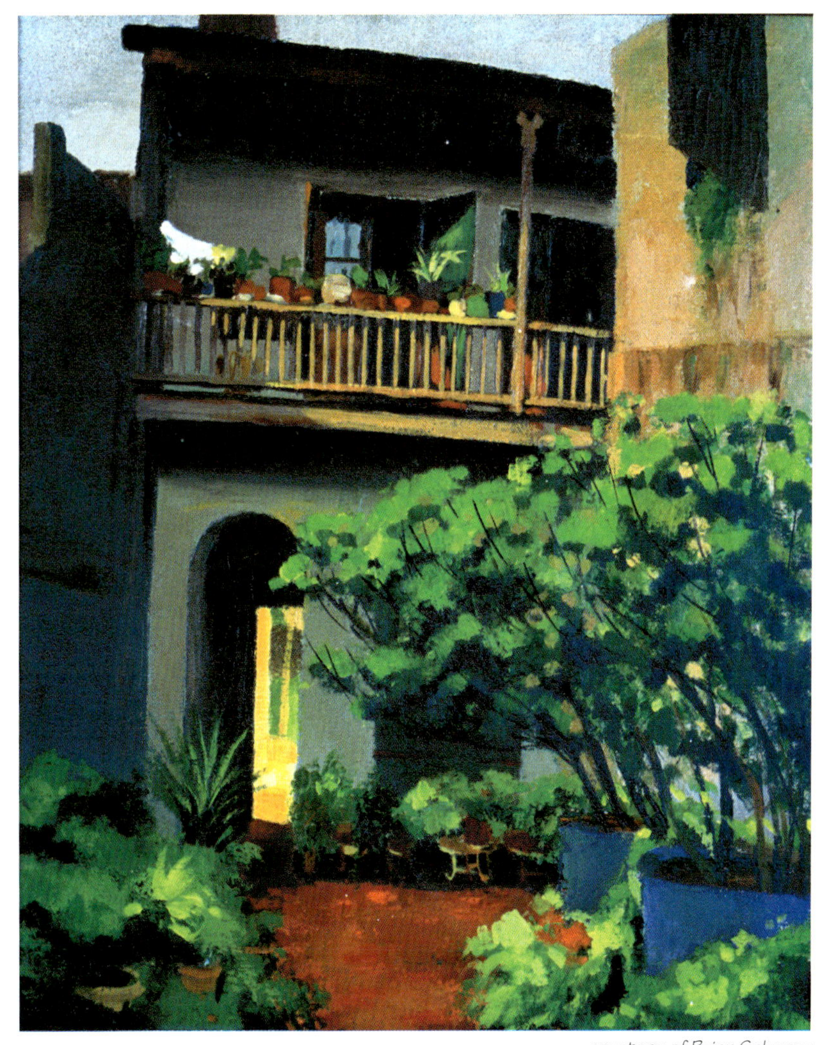

COURTYARD
oil 1946
16x20

At off hours, we explored other parts of New Orleans: City Park, the Delgado Museum, the Garden District, although we took not one streetcar ride, not even the one named Desire. Two rather surreal memories remain from those times: One, late one moonlit night, all by ourselves at the closed-for-the-season amusement park on the shore of Lake Pontchartrain a dense, low fog rolled in. Moving in and out of the huge laughing clown heads and leaving the highest loops of the mammoth roller coaster half suspended in the eerie light and silence, it made a memorable scene, but not a paintable one.

The other, also on Lake Pontchartrain: Driving across the 15-mile-long Lake Bridge we came upon a motorist stranded with a flat tire. Always eager to help, Elden immediately got out and changed the tire, refusing to accept the money the rather inebriated driver offered him. The gentleman kept pulling bills from his wallet, ignoring the fact they were skittering away into the Lake. I took a dim view of all of that and I skittered a bit, myself, trying to retrieve those green portraits of Lincoln and Washington before they were lost forever.

We had Thanksgiving dinner with the Jacobs family in celebration of Elden's having finished Mrs. Jacobs' portrait—no small task with their year-old son on the scene. Then we hitched up the trailer and left Louisiana, headed for Florida. When we crossed the 3-mile Pensacola Bay Bridge and saw the porpoises jumping underneath we felt we had arrived!

Elden was always observing, storing away visual memories of the brilliant Florida Panhandle scene: fresh white sand dunes marked only by bird and animal tracks, bright green water near shore, deep blue farther out, and towering thunderheads over the horizon. We had the road practically to ourselves all the way to Panama City.

We stopped at Tallahassee to complete our Christmas shopping and mail packages home. In a letter he wrote while we were there, Elden outlined his idea of getting together a traveling art exhibition—a part of the dream that was to come true ten years later.

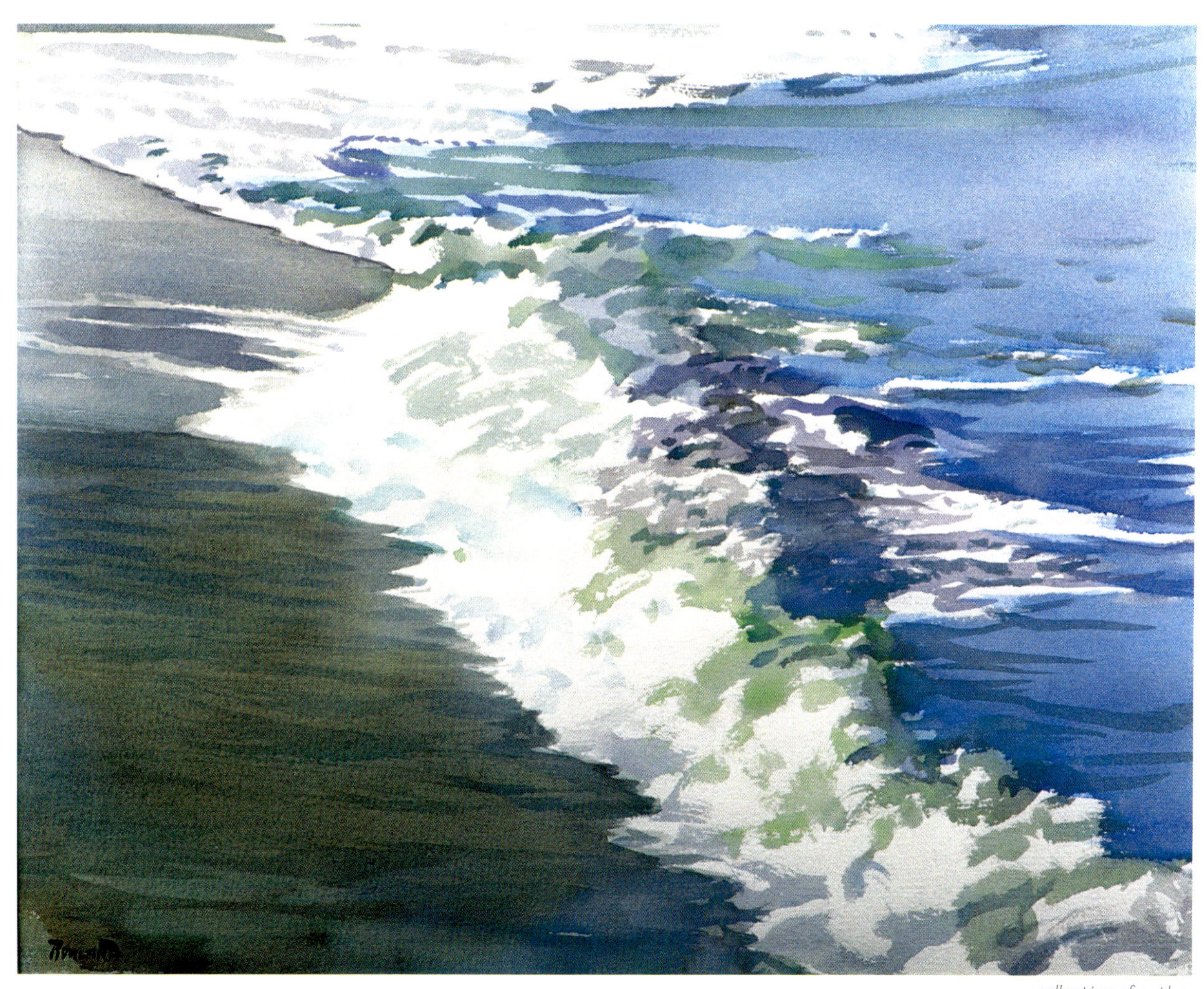

WAVE OF SUBTLE COLORS
watercolor 1980
30x22

Serendipitously, Elden and I found our way to Tower Trailer Court, at Sulphur Springs, near Tampa, for our first winter in Florida—1945-46. The drive south from Tallahassee through Florida's version of fall had prompted Elden to write: "I would have liked to stop and paint, the whole effect is very beautiful, some trees being yellow or red while others are a deep green and all mixed with streamers of gray moss. It was a long, lonesome road with few towns."

We checked out Tarpon Springs, a town of Greek sponge fishermen, and knew we would come back. We went to St. Petersburg and thought that a city of retired persons would probably not be productive of children's portraits to paint, but we did get a good tip about where to park our trailer across the Bay in Tampa.

The owners of Tower Court, Mr. and Mrs. Hensley, were friendly and helpful to us. Before the winter was over they had Elden paint numerous signs they posted to keep their court neat and orderly, had him paint Mrs. Hensley's portrait, and even do a scene for a picture postcard.

When, contrary to our expectations, the weather was not always perfect, Elden would sit in the trailer working on a sample portrait. Another resident saw the work and introduced us to Harry Scott, who wanted to learn to paint portraits. Harry was a personable young man, raised in Costa Rica where his father was an American diplomat. As a child he fell out of a tree, an accident which resulted in the loss of the use of his voice. However, after coming to Tampa, he had speech therapy that enabled him to speak in a low, melodious, mysterious voice with a slow Spanish charm. He promoted Elden's starting small painting classes, had his portrait painted twice, and took us out to drive-in restaurants for shrimp dinners.

The day we met Harry, we also met Bernard and Beatrice Stepner, musicians, waiting to be released from the military. We became good friends, enjoying many hours exploring the West Coast of Florida together, including Sarasota and Tarpon Springs. Beatrice, a pianist, made a beautiful piano recording and exchanged it for a painting Elden did one of the days we were together in Tarpon Springs.

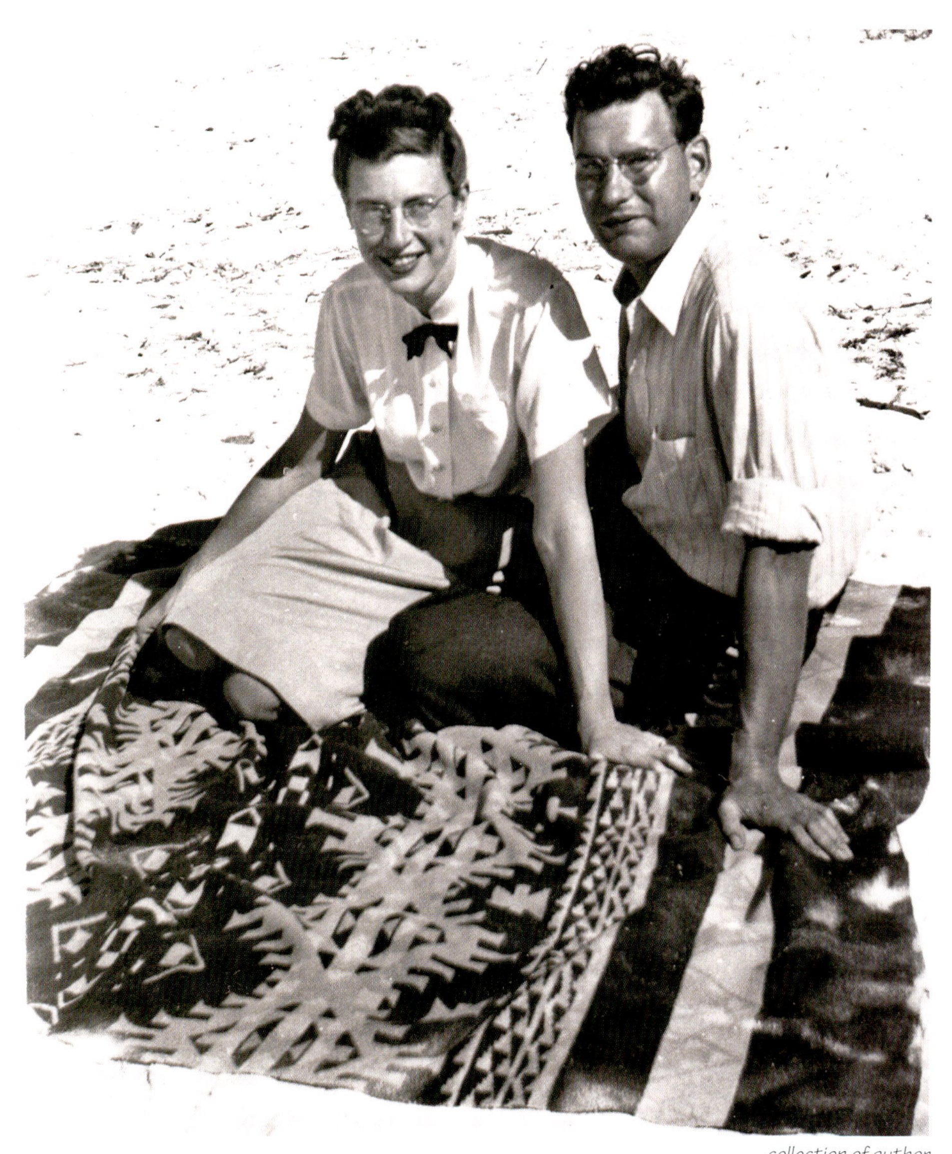

KATHERINE AND ELDEN
photograph 1946

As we had anticipated when we first saw Tarpon Springs, the town with its colorful harbor teeming with little Greek Sponge boats drew us back across Gandy Bridge from Tampa many times. Elden painted small watercolors that were sold from the souvenir shops. He took his students there. The sponge divers felt they knew him so well that when they were short of a person to mind their air hoses, they asked him to fill in. The divers wore heavy metal and glass helmets and cumbersome baggy suits. Whether above water, or below, they were dependent on their air hose for survival. It was a great responsibility, and Elden was glad when the usual attendant soon returned.

At Harry Scott's house in Tampa, Elden and three students painted portraits. Eileen Stevens, whom I met through my job at the Tampa Terrace Hotel, posed for them twice, also my father, who came down from Ohio for a visit. Elden wrote: "I've learned a lot since we have been on this trip, and especially I am learning how much I still have to learn." He was struggling to teach what he had never been taught.

On March 7, 1946, we left Tampa headed south to Key West, taking advantage of the Tamiami Trail, pioneer road that had been cut across the Everglades. After Fort Myers, there were swamps with great cypress trees. Then the real Everglades began—vast expanses of grass dotted with islands of small pond cypress. The grasses stretched away to the horizon, crossed by cloud shadows, streaked with sunlight. Great flocks of white herons and ibis rose up and flew into the endless dome of sky. Occasionally we passed a dugout canoe or a palm chiqui of the Seminole Indians. It was awe-inspiring, beautiful, but needed to be studied before it could be painted.

The same was true of Miami and the Florida Keys. The strings of high hotels and sunbathing "snowbirds" along Miami Beach, and the giant banyan trees encompassing masonry walls of failed subdivisions on the mainland, were equally baffling. The drive down the Overseas Highway, alternating between the solid green of mangrove islands and brightly-hued channel waters was mesmerizing and strange. In Key West we had our first Key lime pie.

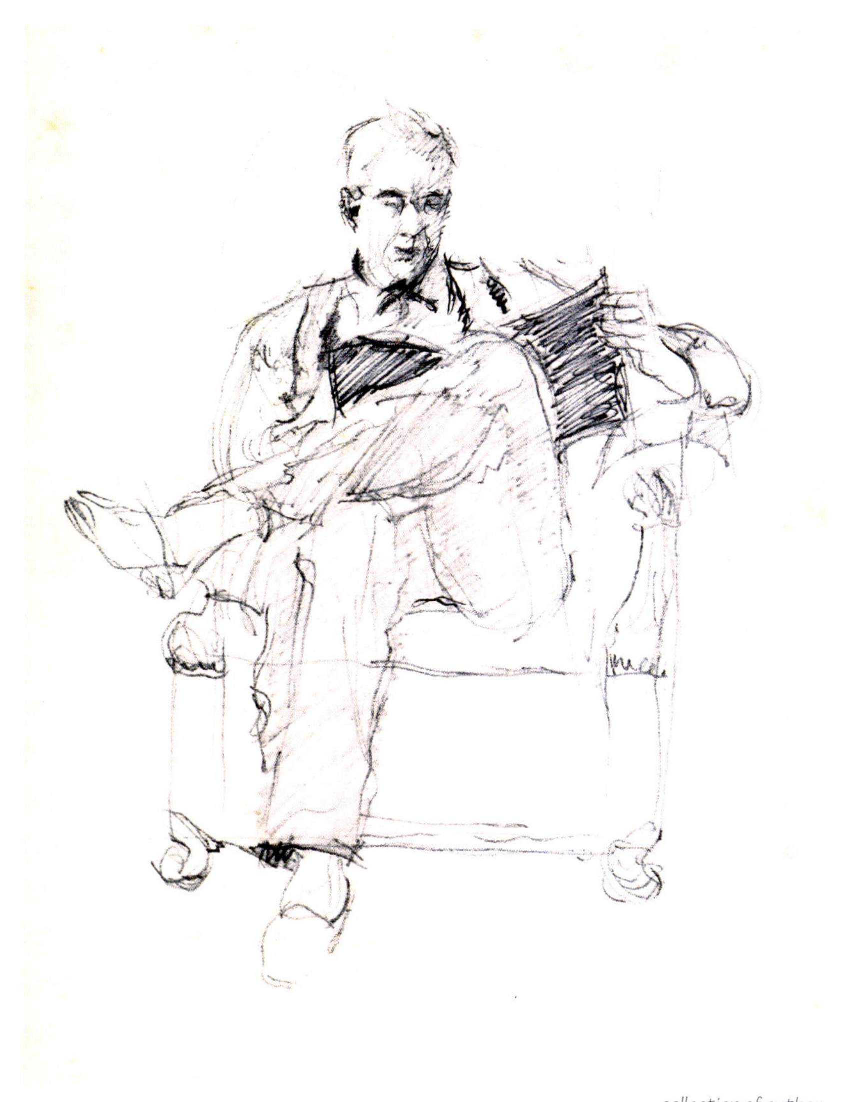

SKETCH OF FATHER
sketchbook drawing 1946
5x7

Reluctantly, on April 1, 1946, we tore ourselves away from our camping spot below the north end of Seven Mile Bridge in the Florida Keys. Although Elden had found the fantastic colors of the Gulf waters and the absolute flatness of the landscape a challenge to paint, it had been fascinating to peer down into the crystal clear waters at sharks, and giant turtles, and fish of all sizes and shapes. The grouper Elden caught had made a delicious meal; the giant Moray eel which I managed to wrestle up to the bridge simply made an enormous splash as he returned to his native habitat.

As we traveled along the coastal highways through Georgia and South Carolina into the mountains of Tennessee and Kentucky, we followed spring north. In that peaceful time, it was easy to find overnight parking spaces for the trailer. One night it was an Atlantic Ocean beach covered with tiny multi-colored coquinas, which we were able to harvest (before they stood on end and quickly wriggled themselves deep into the sand out of sight) for a delicious shell fish broth. One night it was the yard of a

sagging old country church with tall pines dripping festoons of purple and white wisteria blossoms around us. Arriving at Cincinnati, we parked the trailer in the driveway of our house and settled down for a few weeks. Elden got a job doing color separation drawings for a greeting card company. He did a detailed drawing of the Cincinnati skyline as it was then.

One day we went to the Cincinnati Art Museum for what became a life-changing experience. We saw an exhibition of paintings by living artists, collected by Thomas Watson, head of IBM, the big office equipment company. In it was a portrait by Jerry Farnsworth—the head of a young girl, sensitively-painted, beautiful color harmony—and Elden immediately knew he wanted to study with that painter.

We learned about the Farnsworth Summer School at North Truro, on Cape Cod, sent off Elden's application and received word he was accepted. And there was work for me, too, with their friend, Hollywood novelist Robert Nathan.

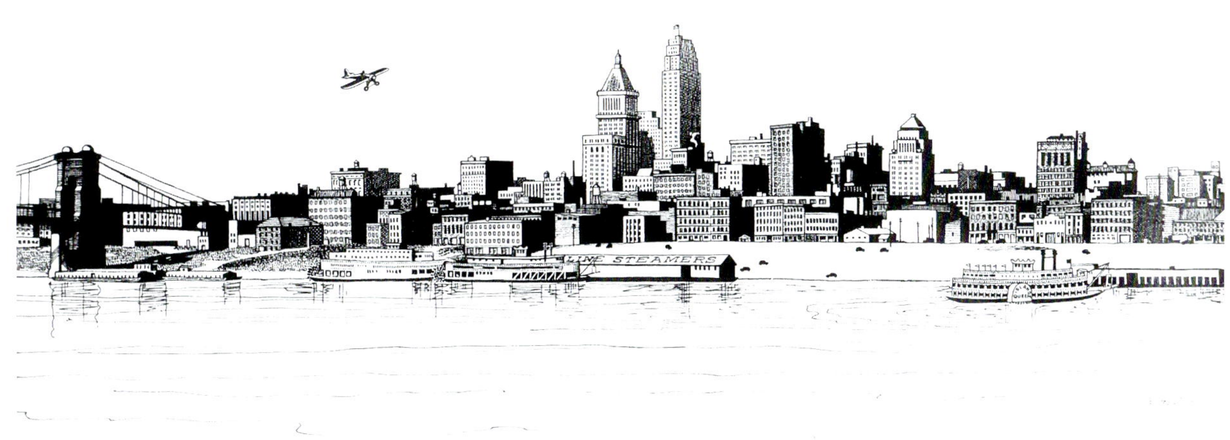

courtesy of Brian Schwarz

CINCINNATI
pen an ink drawing 1946

While we were in Cincinnati I had a temporary job as an "office-sitter." Since all it entailed was infrequent phone calls I had much free time in which to go to the library and get several of Robert Nathan's numerous books. The books, short, gentle, fanciful stories told me much about The Cape, and about the Nathans and the Farnsworths— an exciting preview glimpse into our new world of painters and writers!

We were happy to be back on the road again, traveling through the beautiful vistas of rolling vineyards and cherry orchards of northern Pennsylvania and New York. A fortunate parking one late night at a burned-out fruit stand resulted in our finding ourselves the next morning surrounded by acres of wild strawberries loaded with delicious red ripe little fruits, with which we filled all of the bowls and jars the tiny trailer icebox would hold.

We crossed Cape Cod Canal at about 4 in the afternoon but eagerly pressed on, driving into the sun on the narrow twisting roads. We found a place to park the trailer at the Fire Tower in Wellfleet, and quickly went out to explore The Cape. We began to recognize landmarks from Mr. Nathan's books—the miniature Pamet River, the post office in the tiny town of Truro, and, finally, North Truro itself, with the Farnsworth Studio on the Town Pond. We had arrived!

The fabric of that magical time on Cape Cod the summer of 1946 was woven of many colorful threads: the wonder and gratitude shared by the while nation after being released from long years of intense concentration and deprivation; the spirit of comradeship which remained from those years of everyone working together for the common good; the historic place itself, beautiful in its simplicity and miniature scale; the people, attracted there to live out long-deferred dreams, to teach and be taught at the Farnsworth School of Art—all like the rich hues and textures and shapes of satin and velvet gathered into a colorful crazy quilt, coming together into one creative, harmonious whole.

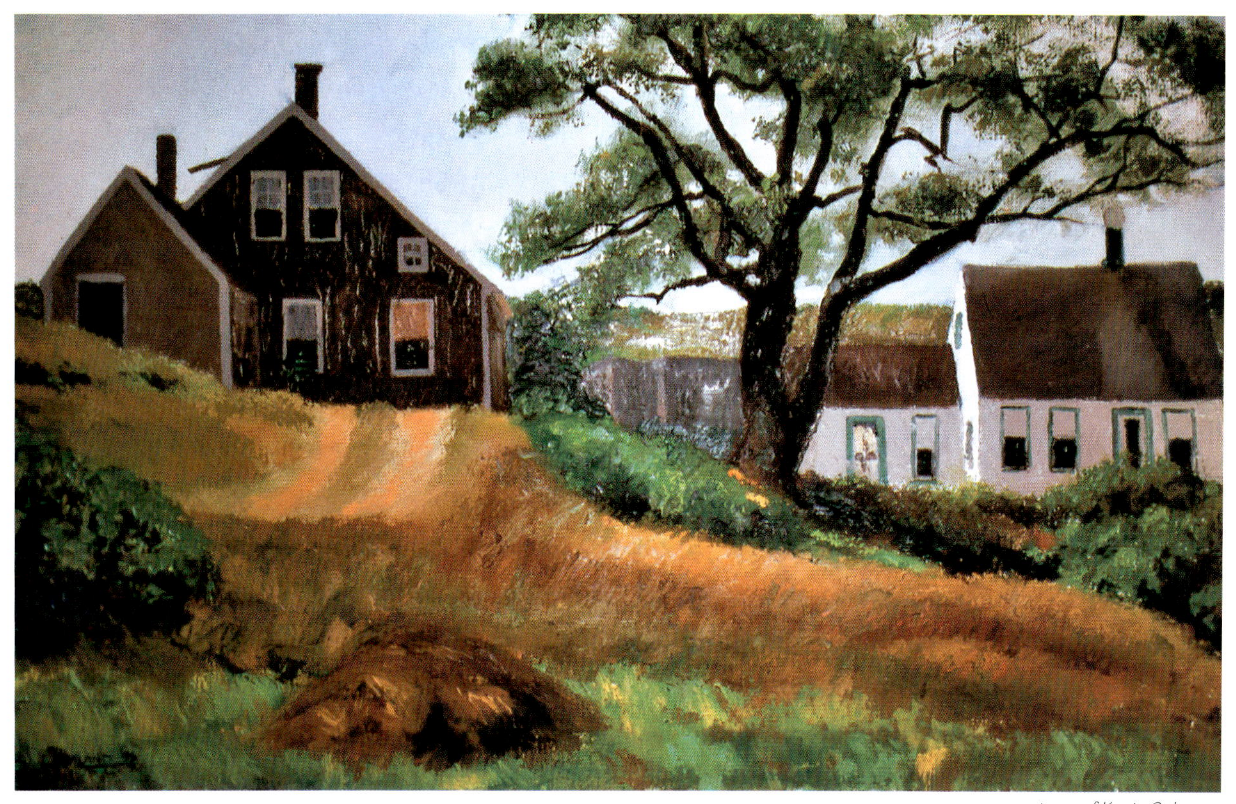

BIG WILLOW
oil 1946
28x20

The "villages" of Truro and North Truro were not so much villages as clusterings of buildings, some silver-shingled, some painted white, nestled among the low sand dunes covered with beach grass and bayberry bushes. Central to North Truro was the little U.S. Post Office, where the students gathered to wait for word from home, and the big gray Farnsworth Art School neatly faced on a long deck cantilevered over a small pond. It all looked like a New England picture post card.

Some distance from the Farnsworth's home stood a huge old house (later known as The Big House) that summer being turned into housing for almost thirty Farnsworth GI students. Next came what had been a two-story carriage house, now occupied by another newly-arrived student, Mrs. Elsinore Budd, and her little dog, Susie.

Just behind that we parked out trailer, and then our car, making a kind of Mother Duck and trailing Baby Ducks line-up. It was great to have such a pleasant, green little valley on the Bay Side in which to settle down for the summer!

I went right to work for Robert Nathan in his attractive home, The Manse, in Truro, a few miles away. He was what I had imagined after reading his books—quiet-spoken, thoughtful—about 45 or 50, smoked a pipe. He was probably best known for his book and movie *Portrait of Jenny* about The Cape and the Farnsworths. He had a delightful study in one wing of the house but often wandered glumly back and forth, ignoring children and guests, and household chores, and me, sitting in the corner of the dining room typing at a portable typewriter on a wobbly card table with Penny, the Cocker Spaniel puppy, nibbling at my toes.

We arrived a few days before the art school was to begin so Elden started digging up a plot of ground by the trailer to make a vegetable garden. He developed blisters, but was proud, finally, to get two neat rows of Patty-pan squash seeds into the Cape Cod sand. He made friends with other students, and they all went off to the Ocean Side to paint High Land Light, still active with resident lightkeeper, whose lonely foghorn was to be our companion all summer.

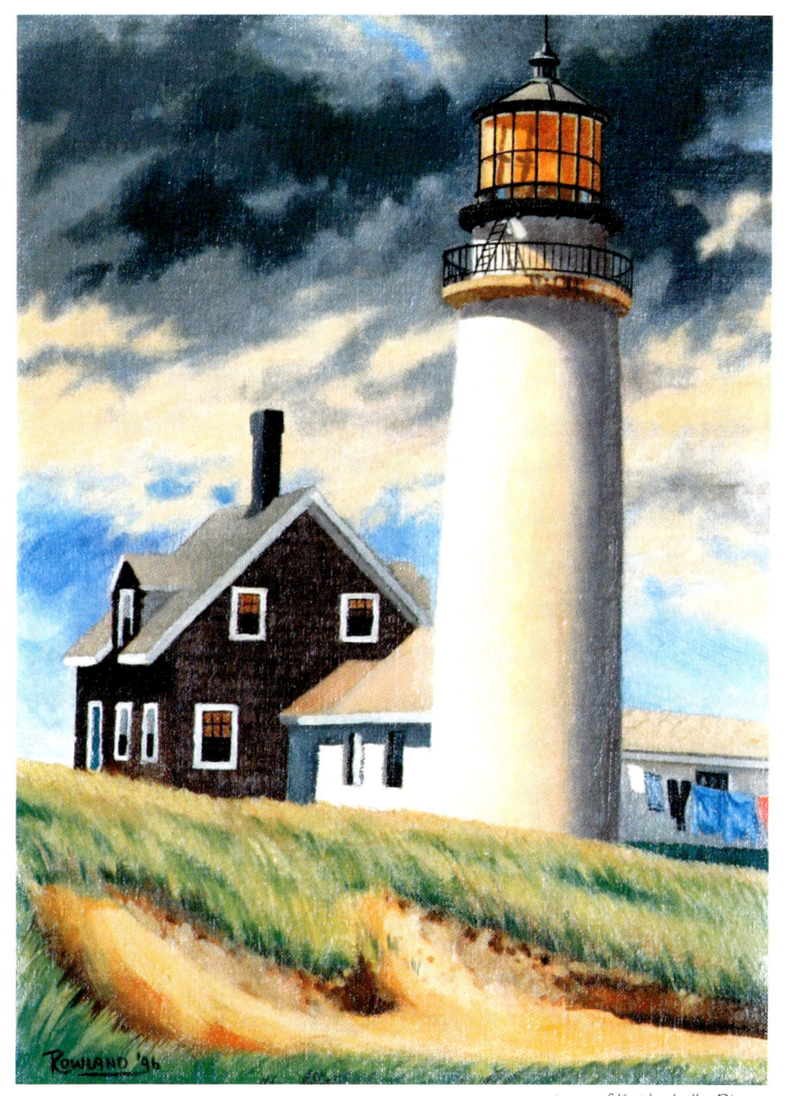

courtesy of Kathy LollarDivens

HIGH LAND LIGHT
oil 1946
12x16

The strong sense of family in our little art community in North Truro revolved around the Farnsworths: Jerry, and, his wife, Helen Sawyer, called by everyone, with respect and affection, Jerry and Henka. Both nationally-known painters at the peak of their careers, gentle, approachable people who were interested in their pupils as human beings as well as students, they continued to influence Elden and me the rest of our lives.

Jerry taught portrait painting, sometimes with as many as four local children posing in the big studio each week. Henka taught still life and landscape. The students worked earnestly five days a week, topped off by the Saturday morning group criticism. Work by each person was put up before the whole class and the audience waited with baited breath to see what Jerry would say.

Elden's first portrait met with terse comment, "Scrape it all off." However, he soon began to understand that putting spots of color together in the appropriate places would result in a vibrant, truthful end result, whether in oil or watercolor, portrait, still life or landscape. He spent

Sunday afternoon, August 19, sitting in the grass painting a 9 x 12 inch oil picture of a Campbell's tomato soup can, with the idea of using all the new ways of thinking and painting he had been learning. The boys in the Big House were all agog, sure Jerry was going to like it. And he did! The smallest picture painted during the entire summer made Jerry say he was humbled to know how he could teach one person so much in one summer.

In-depth study of a book by Jerry and Henka's teacher, Charles Hawthorne, called *Painting with Hawthorne*, also contributed to Elden's improvement, and his habit of observing carefully, retaining what he saw, and thinking innovatively, made possible his fast progress from a commercial artist to a painter.

Late in August, two *Life Magazine* staffers came to make photographs for an upcoming issue on Cape Cod art schools. They pictured all the students on a hillside painting from a nude model. Never mind that Jerry's students never worked that way, it made a good cover the magazine, and later, a book by Jerry.

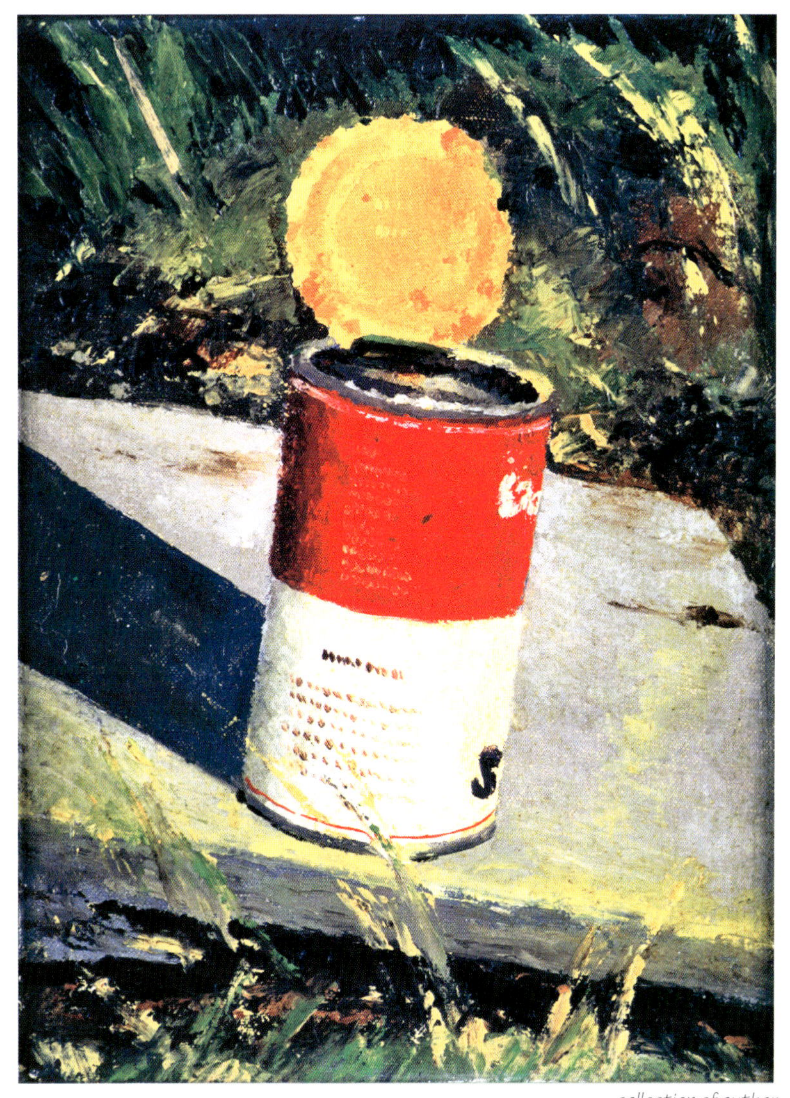

TOMATO SOUP CAN
oil 1946
9x12

The dust cover of *Painting with Jerry Farnsworth* published by Watson Guptill in 1949, carried the *Time Magazine* photograph of the Farnsworth students. I have happy memories of kibitzing from the hilltop with Kathleen Sawyer, Henka's mother, when the photo was taken.

Most of the art schools featured in the *Time Magazine* article were in Province-town, eight miles beyond North Truro, at the tip of Cape Cod. Provincetown played an important part in our lives that summer. The renowned Provincetown Art Association's exhibitions changed monthly. The boys from The Big House were always eager to catch a ride with us to go to spend hours carefully looking at the work of some of the best painters of the U.S.

Meat, and even fish, was hard to get that first year after the end of World War II. The Big House students would appear at the trailer door, list in hand, hoping for a ride to Provincetown. Elden, always willing to help, was glad to oblige, or offer my services as driver. We often laughed about how popular Elden was that summer because he had a car, and a wife who could cook.

On some days the narrow, congested streets would be jam packed with over a thousand day trippers who came from Boston by boat to mingle with the native Portugese fisherfolk and famous artists such as Hans Hoffman and John Whorf. We were always glad to return to our quiet bit of North Truro.

The boggy area below the spot where the trailer was parked was full of blueberry bushes providing a bountiful harvest, which we spent many productive hours picking in spite of mosquitoes. We shared the blueberries and produce from Elden's garden with Elsinore Budd, our neighbor, with whom we became great friends.

The weather, always a predominant feature on Cape Cod, resulted in wildly-fluctuating mood changes among the artists. Many a sunny day landscape had to be changed because the fog, or a nor'easter, came in and stayed for days on end. However, when skies were clear, days, and nights, were unbelievably beautiful. Away from city lights, we saw a brilliant display of aurora borealis one night during a party at the Studio.

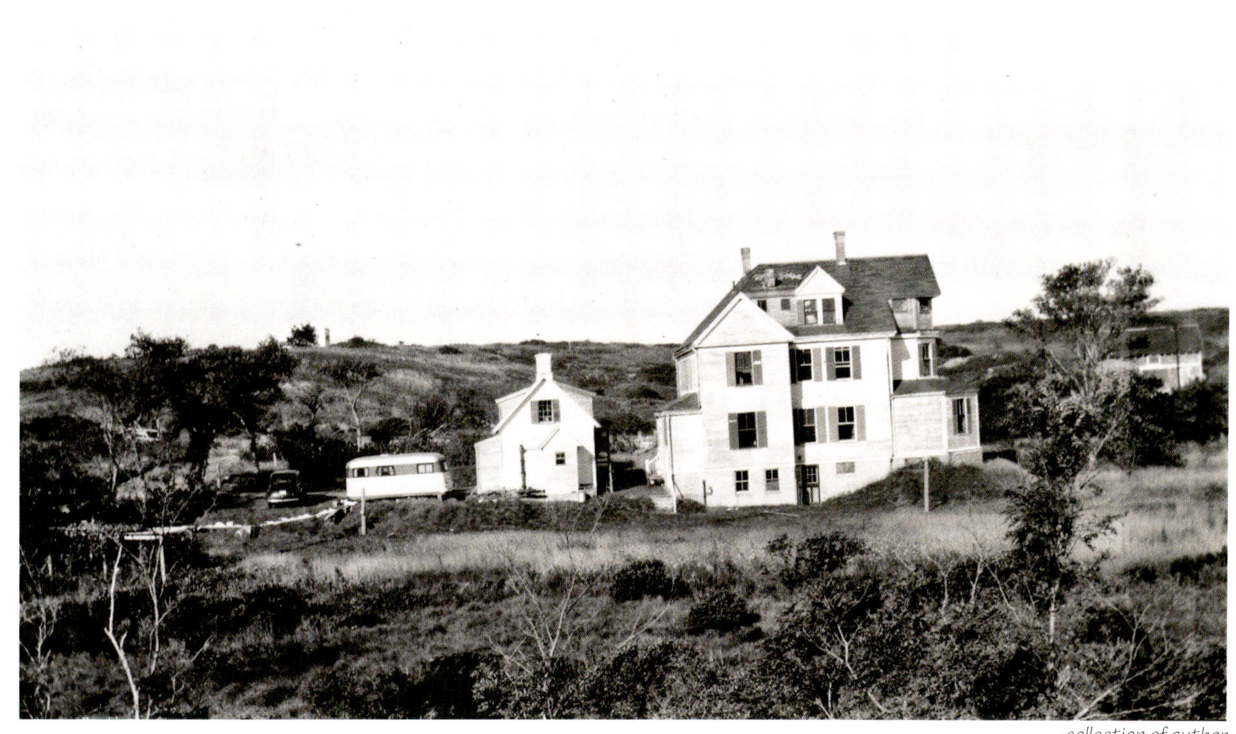

BIG HOUSE AT NORTH TRURO
photo

Robert Nathan's book, for which I typed manuscript that summer of 1946, moved along with astonishing speed, with the whole manuscript completed in a month! On June 29 he gave me the first pages of a draft in long hand on a yellow legal pad into which he had scratched changes and corrections. While I deciphered those pages into a typed version he went on and finished his first draft by July 17! A week later he had just finished his revision when he learned that his publisher, Alfred A. Knopf, needed the completed copy right away so I finished it by July 30 and we sent it off to New York!

Perhaps it is not surprising that the book progressed so quickly. That was the 27th book of prose and poetry that Robert Nathan had produced by that time. The speedy progress of the book left time for me to type for educator Donald Slesinger and to pose in my bright plaid taffeta blouse for Elden and a small group to paint in the Big House. Mr. Farnsworth said he felt Elden and one other boy had made the most progress of the whole class of over 100 that summer.

There was much discussion about the title of Mr. Nathan's new book and a decision had not yet been made when we left The Cape after Labor Day. It was not until the next spring when we made friends with two young women who had advance notice of book releases through their bookstore in San Antonio, that we learned that the title was *Mr. Whittle and the Morning Star*.

The theme dealt, as did all of Mr. Nathan's books, with human emotions and frailties, around the story of Mr. Whittle, a history professor in a small college who thought the world was going to come to an end as a result of the recent discovery of the atomic bomb.

During the summer Elden found numerous ways to indulge his passion for helping other people. The ultimate opportunity came when we packed the trailer and left The Cape, taking with us to New York not only a painting for a student but also a painter in person, Margaret Myrwang, the only female in the Big House, eligible as a GI because she had been a nurse.

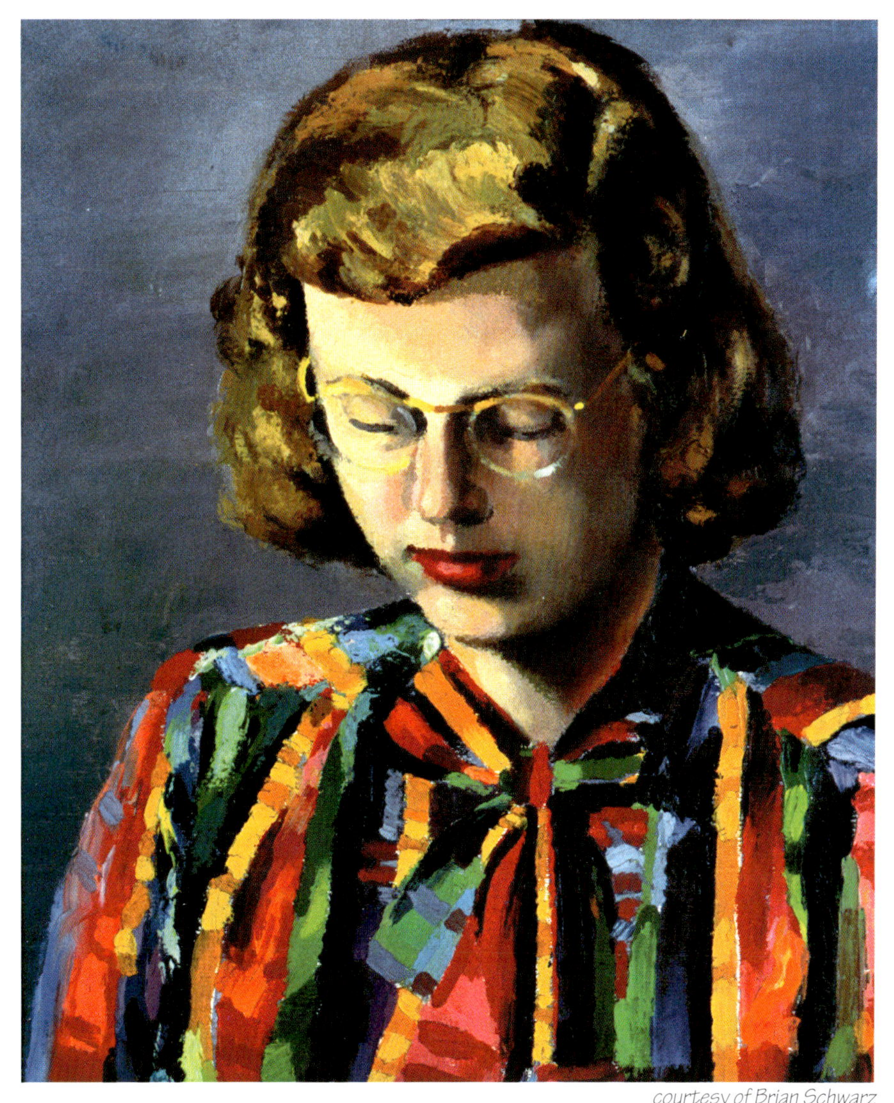

BRIGHT TAFFETA BLOUSE
oil 1946
16x20

We found a place to park the trailer on the Jersey side of the Hudson and commuted into the city for our first look at the Mecca for all budding artists. The first day in New York City is always a never-to-be-forgotten experience. From early morning when we climbed to the top deck of a Fifth Avenue bus until we left the bright lights of Times Square late that night, it was a continuous thrill.

From a Helen Sawyer flower painting in the window of the Milch Gallery on 57th Street, to the Museum of Modern Art where we saw the painting on which Honore Sharrer had worked all summer long in a chicken house in North Truro, to attending a live television broadcast at the invitation of another Farnsworth student, to Cleopatra's Needle in Central Park, the scene of one of Robert Nathan's books—it was an active, memorable four days.

On our way South we spent two weeks in Williamsburg, Virginia. Since neither William and Mary College nor the Williamsburg Foundation, the only employers in town, needed temporary office help at the time,

Williamsburg was the only place in all our trailer travels that I could not find work. Elden took advantage of the beautiful fall weather and the picturesque street scenes. As he sat on the corner finishing an oil of the recently-restored Cole Shop, Richard and Katherine Paquette came along and bought it. However, they agreed to let Elden ship it to them in Seattle, Washington, after he sent it to the Art Association of New Orleans 46th Annual Exhibition. This plunged him into the complicated business of showing in competitive exhibitions, which is such an important part of an artist's life.

 The painting of Cole Shop was accepted in the New Orleans show and the following spring when my mother and father came to see us in New Orleans we were able to show it to them hanging in the Delgado Museum. Elden did not have such good luck when he sent the "Old Mulberry Tree" to Audubon Artists in New York. However, the painting remains a poignant reminder of the early colonists' attempt to produce silk fabrics, the leaves being necessary to feed the silkworms.

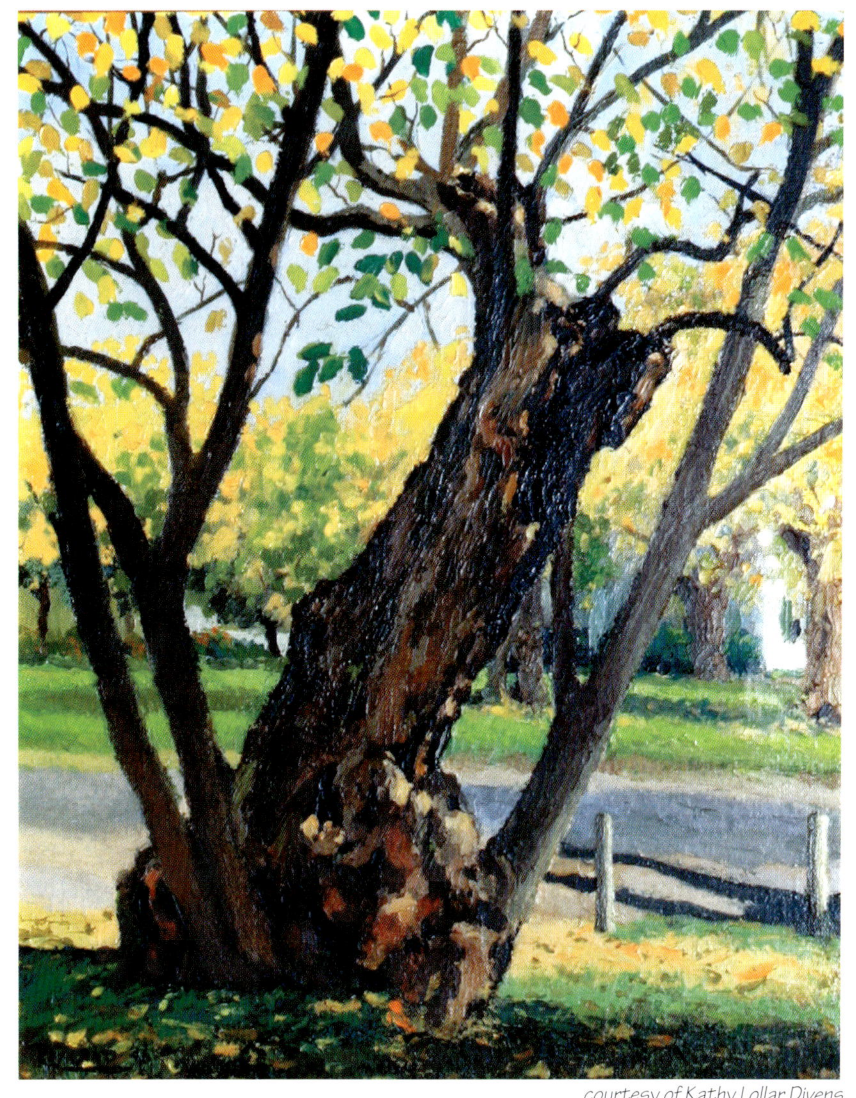

courtesy of Kathy Lollar Divens

OLD MULBERRY
oil 1946
13x16

When we left Williamsburg early in
November of 1946, we were headed for
Tampa so Elden could paint Harry Scott's
portrait. Travel through the Deep South
was picturesque, and interesting. In the
Dismal Swamp, canal boat traffic took
precedent over car traffic so draw bridges
remained open over the water-ways,
closed on demand for land vehicles. Cars
were far outnumbered by small two-wheeled
mule-drawn carts which had their own
pathways along the pavement pulling loads
of cotton, or soy beans, or children going to
school. We even saw several carts pulled by
oxen, fat long horned beasts plodding along
within sight of the skyline of Charleston,
South Carolina.

In Tampa, Elden's portrait of Harry Scott
went well, but slowly, because Harry had
so little time to pose. Elden decided to
get photographs of all of his paintings, an
invaluable practice which he followed the
rest of his career.

I found work at Maas Brothers Department
Store. While I waited for a secretarial

position to open, I filled in at a highly-
advertised sale of an item still very hard to
find so soon after the end of the war—men's
underwear—at 33 cents a pair. Facing a mob
of women frantically waving packages of
men's undershorts made me want to run and
hide, but I didn't—there was a bonus for
the one who sold the most.

After Thanksgiving dinner with the Scott
family, we left Tampa for New Orleans.
Dodging wandering cows and pigs and goats
made driving an adventure in North Florida,
where Open Range Laws were still in effect.

In New Orleans, Elden went to work
painting in the French Quarter, but he felt
he needed to learn about composition. He
went to galleries and museums, and studied
all the art books he could get. In a letter
December 24, he said, "In addition to
color, a painting has to be based on good
active design. I think the works of Picasso,
Matisse, and Cezanne are good to study
for design. Picasso is particularly good,
as he is constantly experimenting and
inventing. No other painter can show the
variety of Picasso.."

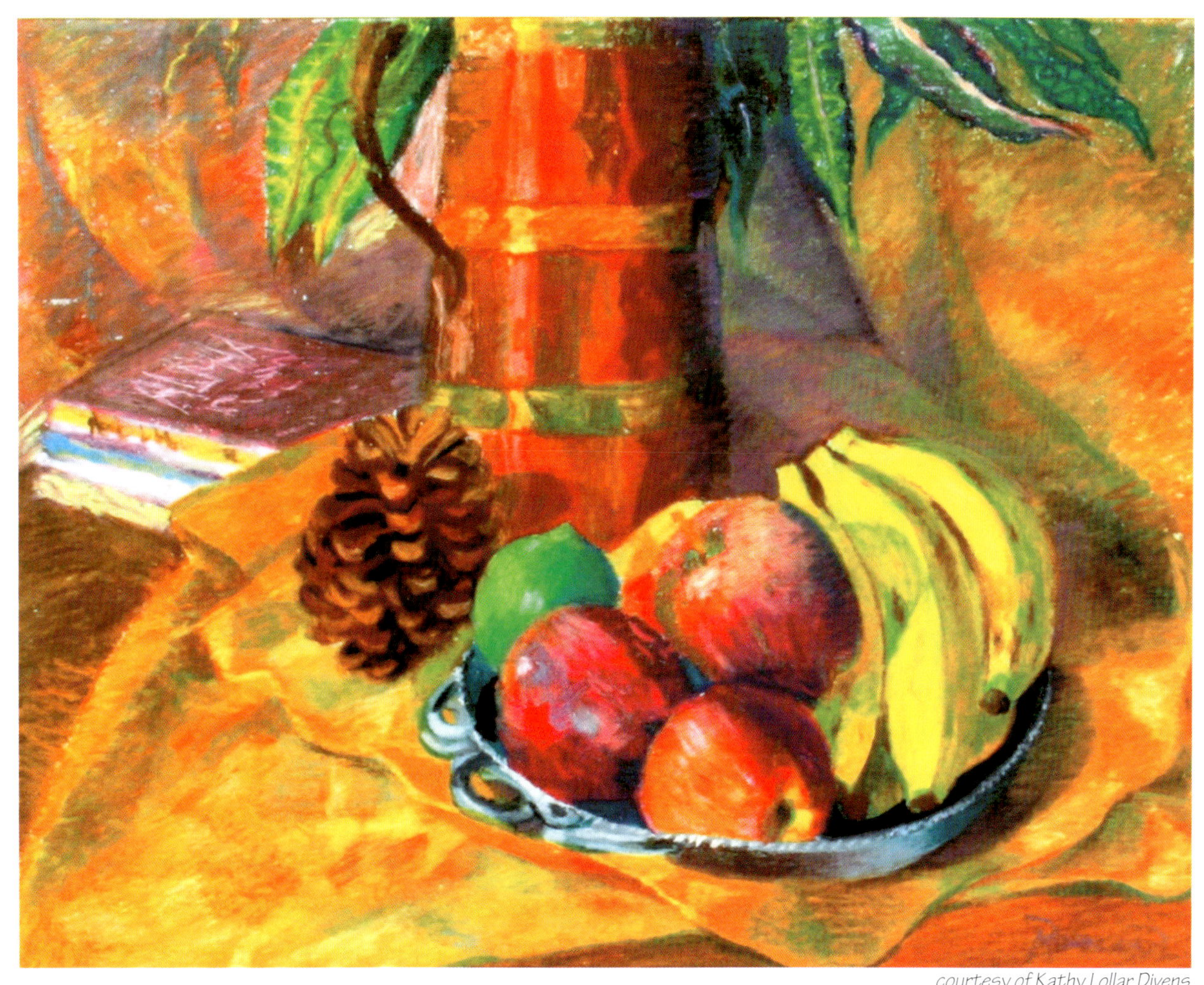

STILL LIFE WITH COPPER PITCHER
oil 1947
20x16

On January 7, 1947, Elden and I pulled our trailer out of New Orleans and drove north to Baton Rouge to cross the Mississippi River on our way to San Antonio, Texas. North of San Antonio we found an ideal place for the trailer. Its location among small ranches surrounded by low rolling hills made it one of the most pleasant sites we ever had. The rhythmic squeak of the windmill, and the chiming of the carillon bells at the Woodsmen of American Hospital not quite a mile away, gave a sense of peace and tranquility.

Elden soon discovered the San Antonio Art Institute, operated by Mrs. Marion Koogler McNay, a wealthy oil heiress, at her home, a Spanish Colonial Revival-style mansion. Elden registered to take classes for a week because, already thinking of someday having his own art school, he wanted to see how the school was operated. He decided not to register for a second week of classes but continued to work on an oil painting of the patio. There Mrs. McNay sought him out and said she had seen his work and wanted to offer him free tuition for a month with Etienne Ret, a French modern teacher

starting the next week. In return she was to be able to choose one of his paintings for her use in the school brochure. Elden took advantage of the offer although he didn't really like Mr. Ret's way of toning every canvas with washes of ochre or umber. From the fourteen paintings Elden did, Mrs. McNay selected a landscape showing rooftops marching up a San Antonio hillside, and impulsively reached in her pocket and gave him its contents: a package of Chesterfields and $9 in cash, "to buy more canvas." Only three years later, Mrs. McNay died, leaving her estate and fortune to start the Marion Koogler McNay Museum.

My job at the Graduate Nurses' Association was fun. Mrs. Brown, the manager, fed me tea and cookies and entertained me with stories of her younger days when she rode in a women's polo team. She insisted that Elden and I should go to Mexico. By a coin toss we chose Eagle Pass over Laredo and walked across the Rio Grande River Bridge to Piedras Negras and at once realized we were in a different world when we met a man on his way to market carrying ten dead chickens around his neck.

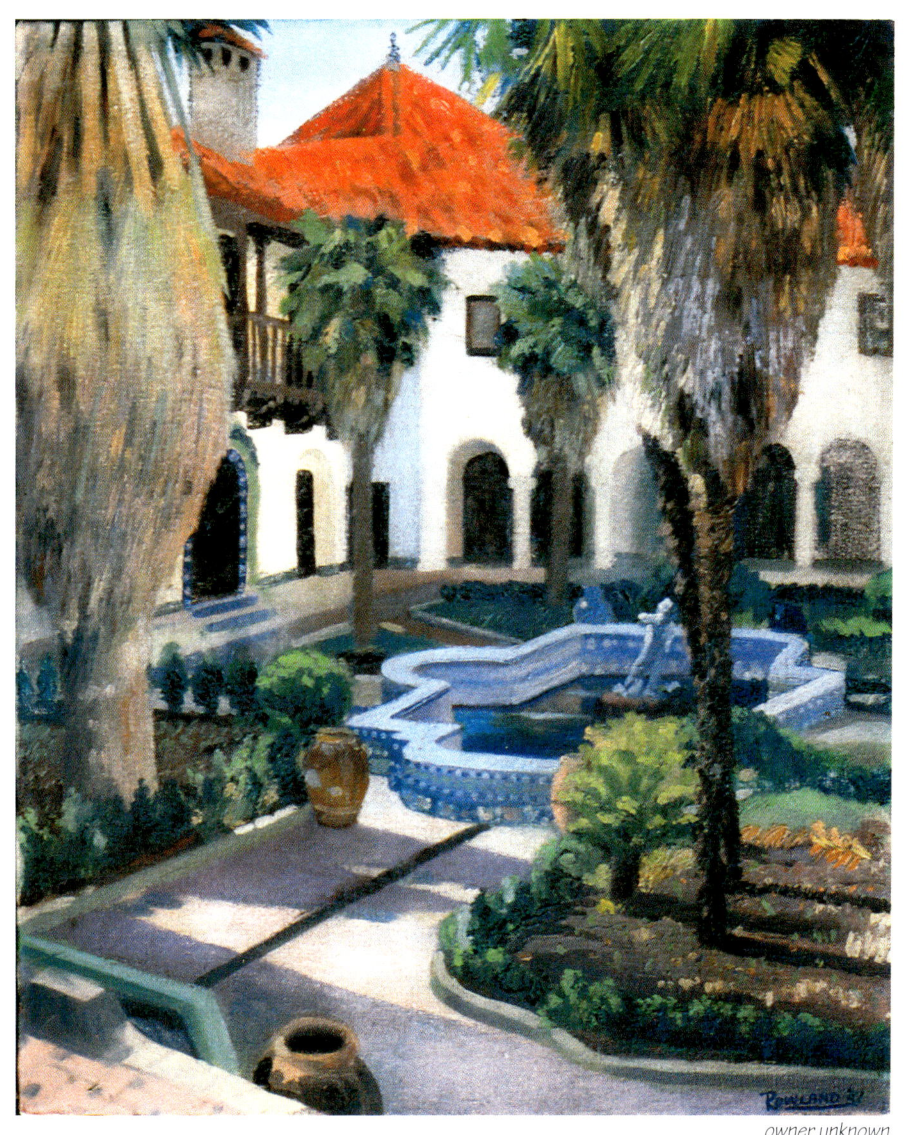

SAN ANTONIO PATIO
oil 1947

In the first days of March 1947, Elden and I left San Antonio heading back east to New Orleans. In Louisiana our route followed Bayou Teche, center of the land about which Longfellow wrote *Evangeline*. Elden was beginning to concentrate on watercolor paintings in anticipation of a hoped-for show at Clossen's in Cincinnati. The little gray unpainted buildings sitting along the bayous, lines of washing blowing in the breeze, surrounded by huge live oak trees dripping moss and brightly-colored azaleas and delicate camellias, made ideal subjects for the speedy watercolor medium. Stopping along the road, even in the rain, Elden painted in the front seat of the car. Between the Intracoastal Waterway and the Southern Pacific Railroad, our car bounced up and down like a boat on water.

In a very full ten days in New Orleans we showed my parents the sights of the area and took them to visit Alberta Kinsey who had taught at the Lebanon, Ohio, Normal School when my mother went there. We went picnicking with our friends John and LuNeal McReavy and Elden painted oil portraits of both of them.

From New Orleans we moved our traveling home base north to a spot high on a bluff over the Mississippi River, in Natchez, where the Annual Spring Pilgrimage was in full swing. Over thirty ante-bellum mansions were opened by their owners for thousands of tourists to visit for a designated fee. We followed the purple route markers so Elden could select the ones he wanted to paint. He chose Auburn, and Rosalie, and Longwood.

Although not as old as Auburn (1812) and Rosalie (1820), the architecture and story of Longwood (1860-61) was especially intriguing. Construction of the house was under way when owner and workmen all went off to the Civil War (we were reminded that the proper term is "War Between the States.") The octagonal red brick structure topped by an onion dome was spectacular, the fact that the upper floors were exactly as the workmen left them three-quarters of a century before was touching. To cope with the congestion, Elden made mental notes and photos as source material from which to paint later, setting a precedent for his subjective painting style.

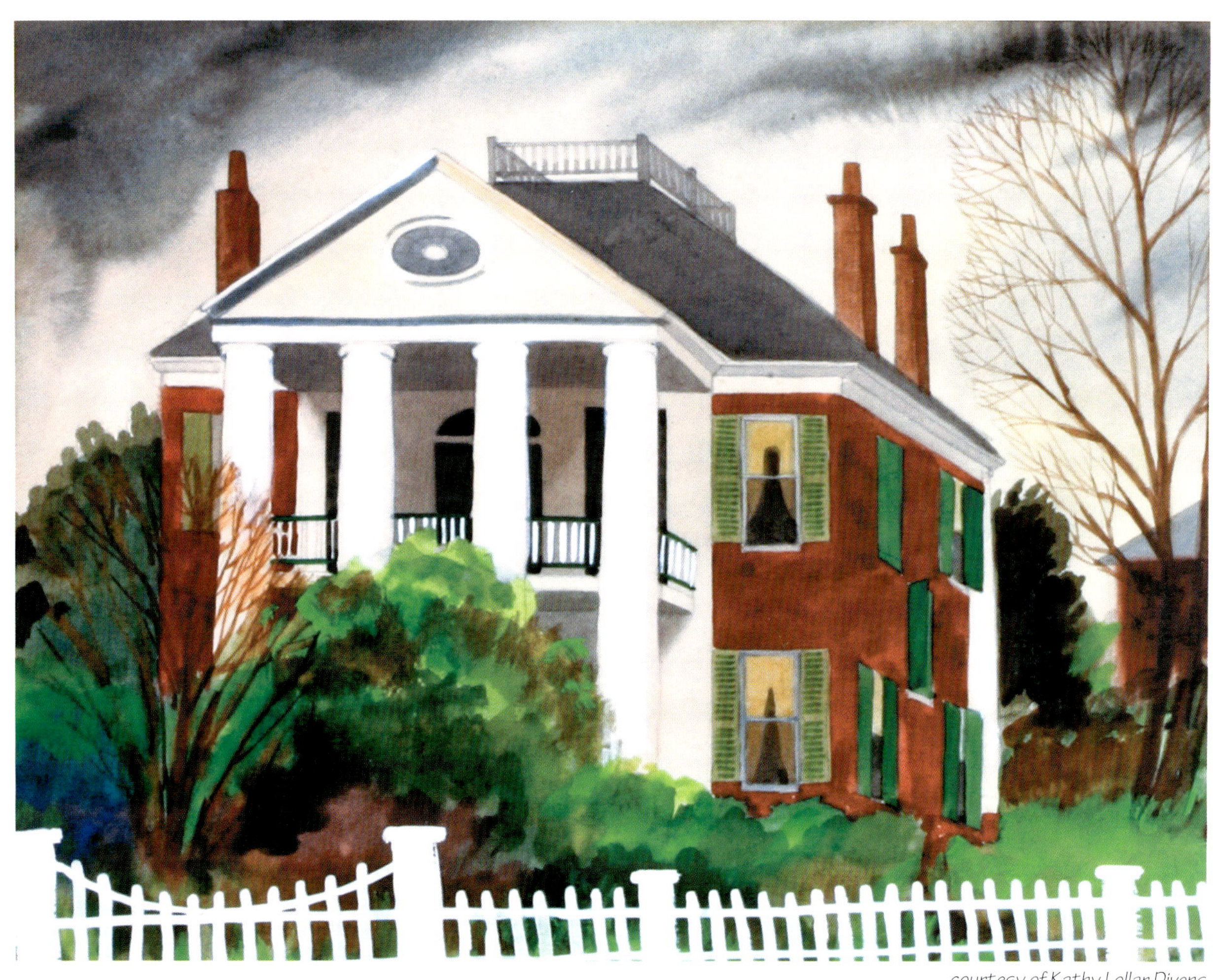

ROSALIE AT NATCHEZ
watercolor 1947

33

Elden had decided to spend the summer of 1947 studying with Robert Brackman in Noank, Connecticut. In he meantime, he was pouring over all the art books he could find. He spent hours studying the book on the French Impressionists, that he received for his birthday, May 31. We packed as many galleries and museums as possible into a two-day visit to New York.

At Noank, we wiggled our way around boulders in Mrs. Brown's cow pasture to situate our trailer on the shore of Long Island Sound, and went to see Mr. Brackman who had recently finished a portrait of Jennifer Jones for the movie, "Portrait of Jennie," produced by David O. Selznick. She had come to Noank to sit, and had caused quite a stir in the little town. To us, it seemed strange that Mr. Brackman was chosen to do the picture, because Robert Nathan, for whom I worked the previous summer, had written the book with Jerry Farnsworth in mind.

Mr. Brackman criticized all the students' work severely, causing one student we knew to go home to Sarasota. Elden simply withdrew from the studio into an empty rock quarry or painted around the farm. However, two small oils he did, "New England Rocks" and "Boats in Sunlight," were later exhibited in the American Artists Professional League's show in the National Museum at the Smithsonian.

I worked in the stenographic pool of the U. S. Navy Underwater Sound Laboratory at New London. Civil Service rules seemed unfair to temporary workers. However, I loved riding on a tiny local bus to get to the Laboratory, bouncing along on narrow country roads between stone walls laden with masses of honeysuckle and rambler roses. I enjoyed learning about new things like "sonar" and "radar" and having picnic lunches on the dock with a view of the magnificent sailing vessel *Eagle* anchored in the Thames River at the Coast Guard Academy nearby. One morning as I arrived, other workers excitedly reported that a body had been hanging from the yardarm of the *Eagle* and was cut down to fall into the water. Actually, it was a dummy, a traditional ritual when a new class graduated from the Academy.

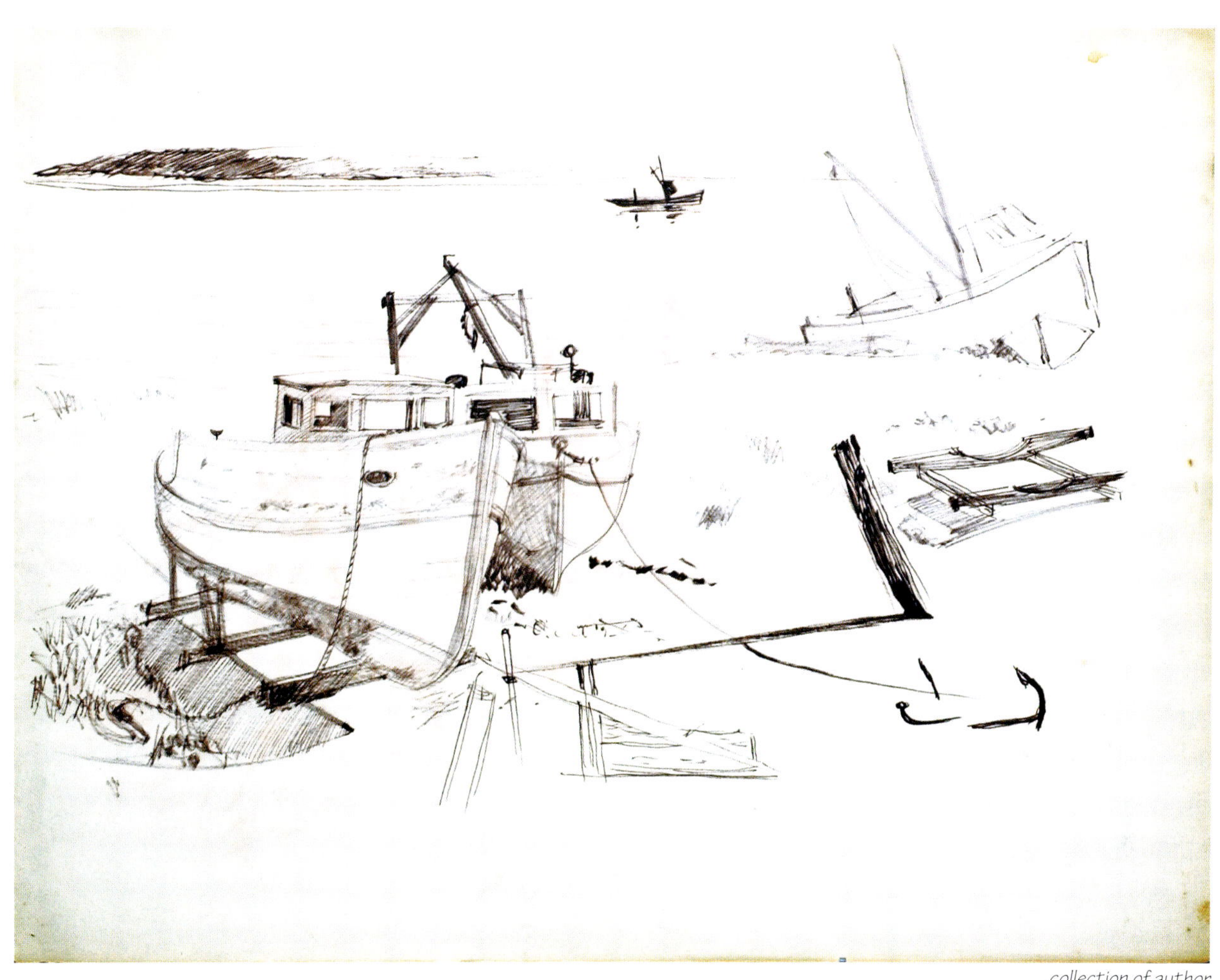

collection of author

BOATS IN SUNLIGHT
sketchbook
13x18

At the urging of Mrs. Cecil Hunker, we went to the Washington, D. C., area in the fall of 1947 and accompanied her when she registered for a fall course at the Corcoran Art School. While there, Elden arranged to pose at a portrait class.

To pose, Elden went in his blue jeans and sport shirt, which made Mr. Lahey, the Director of the School, decide that he should pose him standing with his arms folded and peering into a corner in a rugged looking manner. In his demonstration, Mr. Lahey pointed out what he wanted the students to portray—the stubborn mouth, the determined jaw, the intense and sincere eyes, the writhing torment of the hair. He said Elden had a "very fine head." In fact, the whole character analysis was flattering but Elden never quite lived down the "writhing torment" comment.

We went to The Phillipps Gallery located near The Corcoran. We knew that The Phillipps had a famous collection of Impressionst paintings. But nothing could prepare us for the impact of our first never-to-be-forgotten sight of Renoir's awe-inspiring "Boating Party"!

We were delighted that Elden's painting "Broken Cup" was one of 135 out of 800 accepted for the Artists of Washington and Vicinity show at the Corcoran Gallery and excitedly prepared to attend the opening in early November. In spite of frantic shopping, I did not find what I thought would be an appropriate dress so I went in the light blue and tan plaid wool suit I had made, and Elden brought out his suit. There were some people in evening clothes but most were in clothes such as ours.

In the meantime, I worked in downtown Washington at the Tuberculosis Association addressing envelopes to send out Christmas seals, including one to Harry S. Truman, at the White House. It was piece work. I earned $12 a day, plus blisters on the tips of my little fingers.

We were feeling on top of the world as we left Washington headed for Sarasota and the Farnsworth Art School.

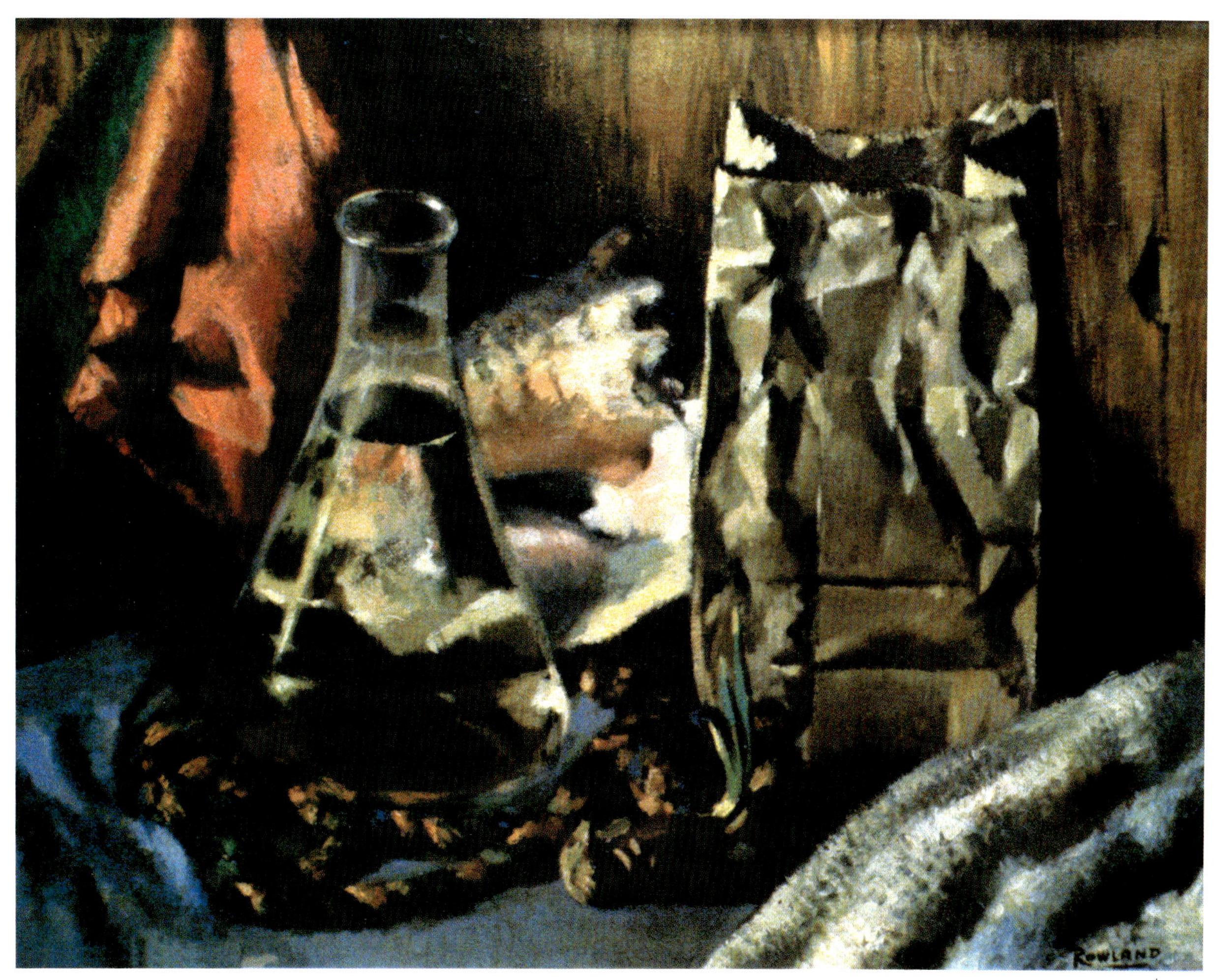

owner unknown

STILL LIFE WITH PAPER BAG
oil 1948
20x16

Late in 1947, Elden and I spent a month in Tampa, so he could paint another portrait of Harry Scott. During that summer, while we were in Connecticut, Elden had arranged to be a monitor in the Farnsworth School in Florida the coming winter, so we headed for Sarasota early in December. My journal entry for December 12 comments, "The distance between Sarasota and Tampa is one solid mass of truck farms. They are picking tomatoes and gladioli now."

We found a place for our trailer south of Sarasota at Pine Shores Park, on Stickney Point Road, not far from the bridge cross-ing Little Sarasota Bay. As the winter wore on, in our trips to the beach on Siesta Key, we grew to know that bridge well. It was of the old style, which was turned sidewise to allow boat traffic, rather than rising into the air as newer drawbridges did. The power to turn the cumbersome structure was provided by a man walking round and round at the end of a long pole. But even that exasperatingly slow process seemed preferable to finding it left wide open, with no barrier across the road, as we did one dark night.

Immediately after we arrived at Sarasota we plunged right in to getting settled. On December 12, Elden joined the Sarasota Art Association which was then located at the airport in one of the barracks left from training fliers during World War II. He also began to help with the finish work on the new house the Farnsworths were building on Hanson Bayou on Bay Island.

The Farnsworth art classes, which began after Christmas, were held in another of the barracks at the airport. After that Elden was busy with his duties as monitor: hiring models, transporting, posing and timing them, finding housing for students, keeping the studio clean, stretching canvases, etc., as well as painting and filling numerous sketchbooks.

I found a full time placement as secre-tary to Ralph C. Caples, a wealthy good will ambassador for Seaboard Air Line Railroad and owner of his own advertising agencies in several northern cities. The only qualifications for the job were "to be able to take rapid dictation and to have a sense of humor."

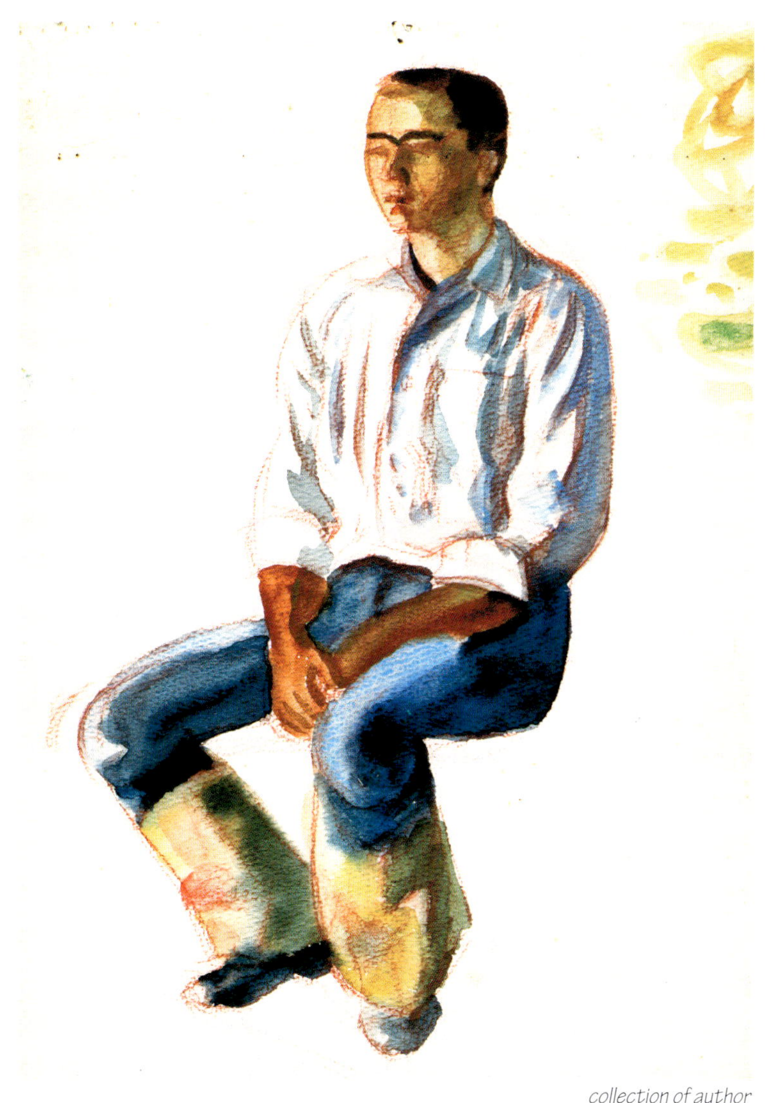

collection of author

BOY POSING
watercolor sketch
8x12

Mr. Caples' office was on the second floor overlooking Lower Main Street, Sarasota. He rarely came into the office, but spent his time working on fund drives for the Salvation Army, or gathering citrus and canned goods to send off to friends and associates in the North, or going on charter boat fishing trips, or simply driving around with Mose Ball, his chauffeur, in his beloved Packard cars, counting Ohio license plates (Ohio was his home state). When he did come charging up the steps he began dictating at break-neck speed. I quickly transcribed the letters, he signed them, and off he went again. In earlier years, he had been influential in having the Ringling Brothers buy property next to his lovely Spanish style home on Sarasota Bay north of town. He adored his petite wife, Ellen, and bought her an orchid almost every day.

This left me much free time, to read, to write personal letters, or knit, or just sit looking out on the street below, often in company with Mose, who waited in the office while Mr. Caples was visiting his cronies. Occasionally, Mrs. Charles Ringling came up and sat dozing, waiting for her chauffeur. Columnist David Lawrence, who had a teletype in a spare room, did not come in.

One evening Elden and I stopped at the Farnsworths' home and met Mrs. Eric Hodgins, starting a chain of events which influenced the rest of our lives. Mr. Hodgins was due in Sarasota in a few days from Hollywood where he had been a consultant on the making of a movie from his best-selling novel, *Mr. Blandings Builds His Dream House*, with Myrna Loy and Cary Grant. Mr. Hodgins needed someone to type an article he was writing for *Life Magazine* about the experience of making the movie. The article had to go off to New York the very night of his arrival, which was Easter Sunday. Would I type the article? Of course, I would.

Eric Hodgins had been the first Editor of *Fortune Magazine* and Eleanor Treacy, his wife, had been the first Art Editor. Eleanor had commissioned Jerry Farnsworth to do artwork for the magazine and had come to Sarasota to study painting with him. That Easter Sunday was the beginning of a long, affectionate association between the Rowlands and the Hodginses, and I became known as "Katie."

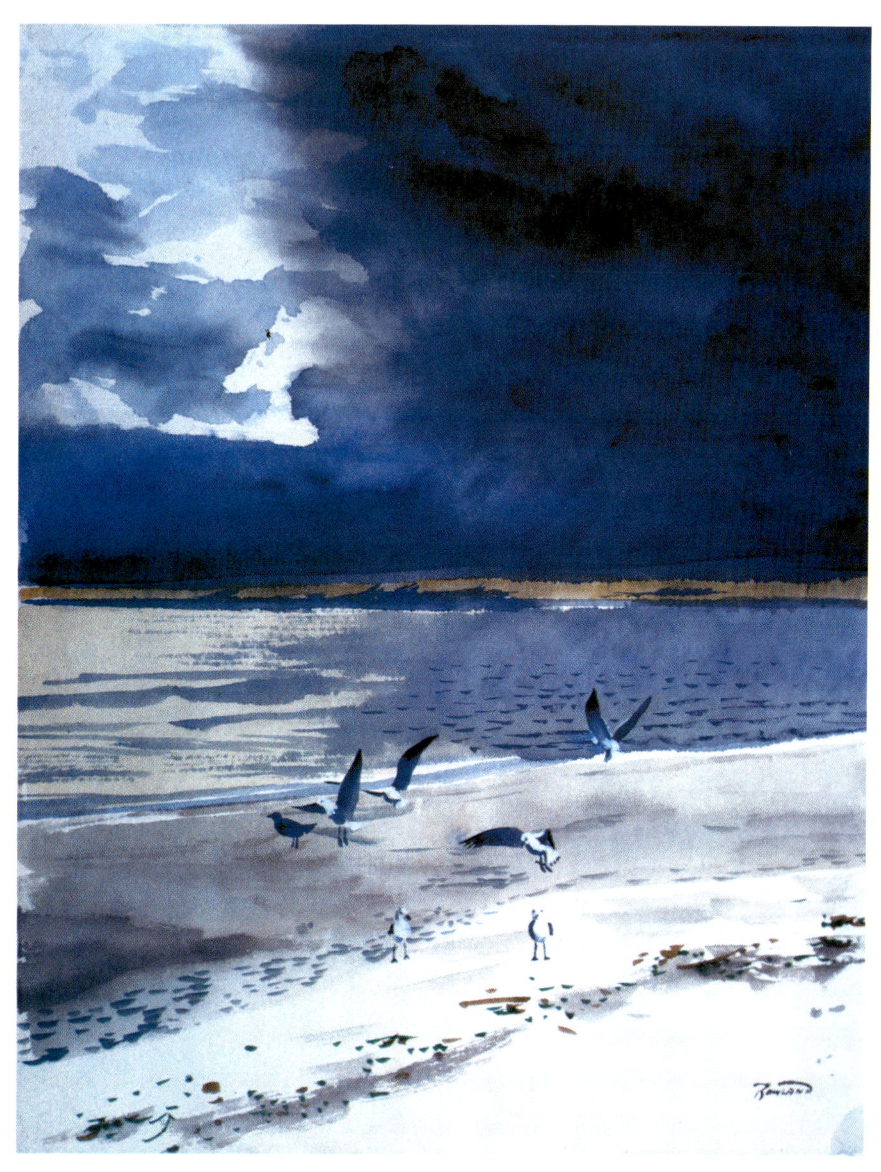

BEACH
watercolor 1981

Elden worked hard at the Farnsworth
School the winter of 1948 finding models
and dealing with their temperaments.
Journal entry on February 28 says, "Elden
is struggling along as usual with his painting.
Right now he is rather discouraged and goes
around in a thick fog of gloom. Not that
there is anything wrong with his pictures:
Mr. Farnsworth says all they need now is
some imagination."

In spite of all of that, he sold ten paintings, and won his first prize in a competitive
exhibition. Harry Scott entered Elden's
portrait of him in the Florida State Fair art
exhibition and it won a second prize of $5!
This tiny "first" pleased everyone except
Elden, who felt the competition was not
good enough.

By early April, after he saw a surrealist
painting at the Ringling Museum by Leonid
Berman (Russian-American, 1896-1976),
Elden began to use his imagination for
backgrounds. The April 7 journal says,
"This girl is going to be seated on a boat
on a beach, and Mr. Farnsworth was very
enthusiastic in his criticism." Thus began

the "Girl on The Beach Series," which
continued for the next six years.

In the meantime, I continued my idyllic
life of working for two dynamic gentlemen
at the same time: Ralph Caples and Eric
Hodgins. When the *Blandings* article
came out in the April 12 issue of *Life*,
Mr. Hodgins gave me a marked copy: "To
Katherine—without whose demon typing
these pages would be blank—with best
regards from Eric Hodgins."

Life in general was fun that winter—Elden's
mother visited us, we made friends, we went
to the beach, we even went fishing, although
I quickly gave up fishing when someone
else caught a fish and I decided I did not
want to have to deal with any such flopping,
gasping creature, to throw back, or even
to eat.

On May 13, Elden came bounding up
the steps at the Caples office bearing
gardenias, ready to celebrate our wedding
anniversary, but I was still busy helping Mr.
Caples gather citrus and watermelon and
corn for him to take North.

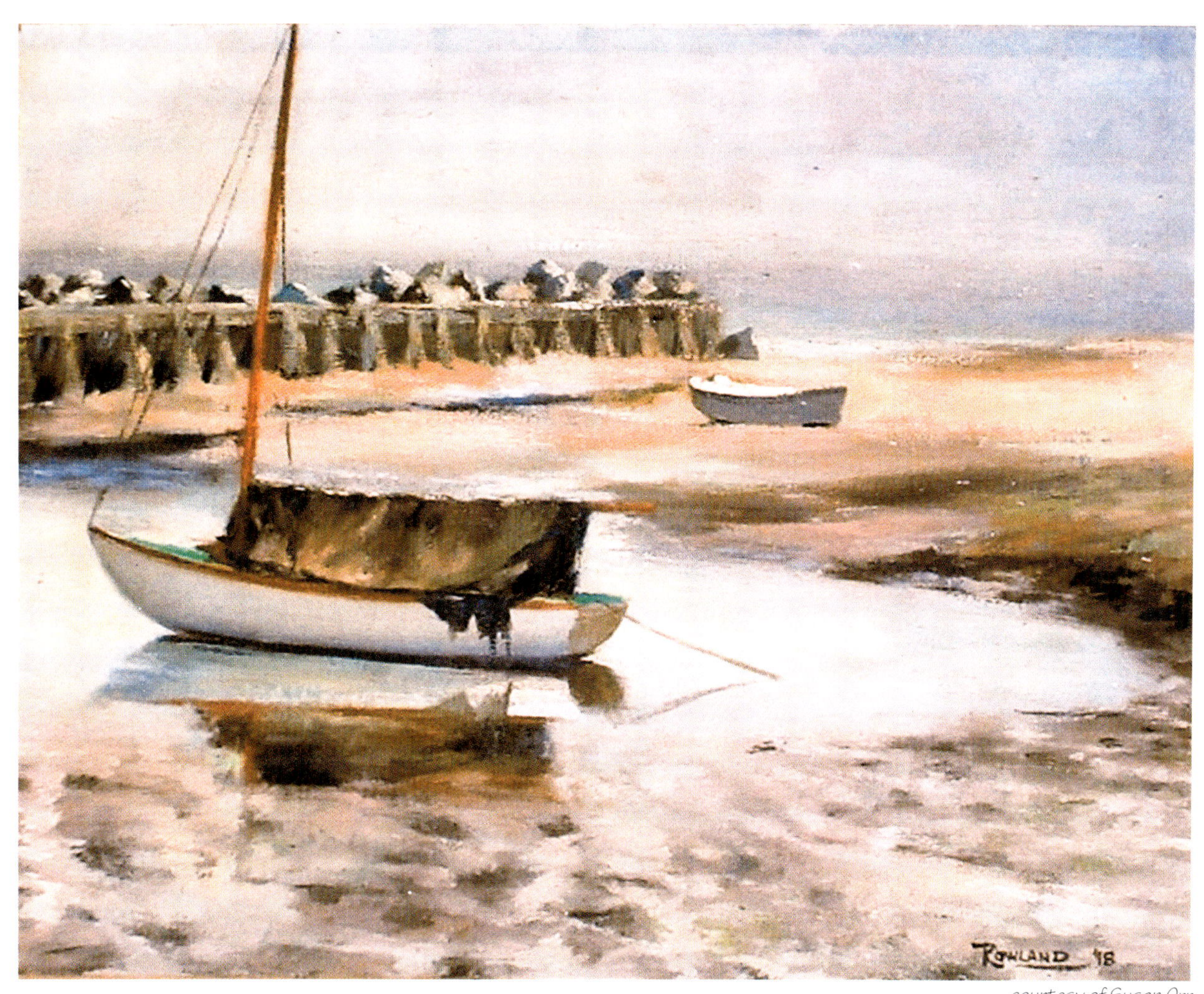

BEHIND THE BREAKWATER
oil 1948
15x19

My last duty for Mr. Caples in the spring of 1948 was to see him and Mrs. Caples off on their trip to New York in a private car sent down by the Seaboard Railroad.

The Hodginses asked me to work for them in East Dennis, on Cape Cod, where Eric would be writing a second *Mr. Blandings* book. Elden decided he wanted to paint on his own that summer, rather than going to an art school. Cape Cod would be a perfect place for him to do that because he could paint independently but take his work to the Farnsworth classes in North Truro for Saturday morning criticisms.

We stayed with our friend Elsinore Budd in Tarrytown, and all went into New York City on the commuter train for several days visiting galleries and art museums. We also saw the fullscale replica of the *Blandings* Dream House which had been built at Fifth Avenue and 44th Street as a fund raiser for the Heart Foundation. When I stopped in at the Caples Advertising Company office I found that Mr. Caples was resting at a hotel, having not been well since he left Sarasota.

When we arrived, the Hodgins family—Eric, Eleanor, son Rod and daughter Patty—was already established in a big house overlooking Cape Cod Bay, at East Dennis. With their help, we soon found a place to park our trailer on Mr. Howes' farm just a ten-minute walk away along the beach. It was a perfect setup for the summer—Mr. Howes' barn had a north-facing loft room for Elden to use as his studio, we had all the facilities we needed for the trailer in a lovely rural setting, and the same gorgeous view that people came from far and wide to enjoy.

Eric went off to Connecticut to take Rod to school and to New York City to take care of duties for Time, Incorporated, of which he was still a vice-president. Elden and I settled into a pleasant routine of painting and posing, and helping Eleanor and 4-year-old Patty who stayed on at The Cape. Elden also helped Mr. Howes put up hay. In his words, "I helped pitch hay twice, both times it fell off, once in the barn."

I was pleased to be free to pose for "Girl on the Beach" paintings.

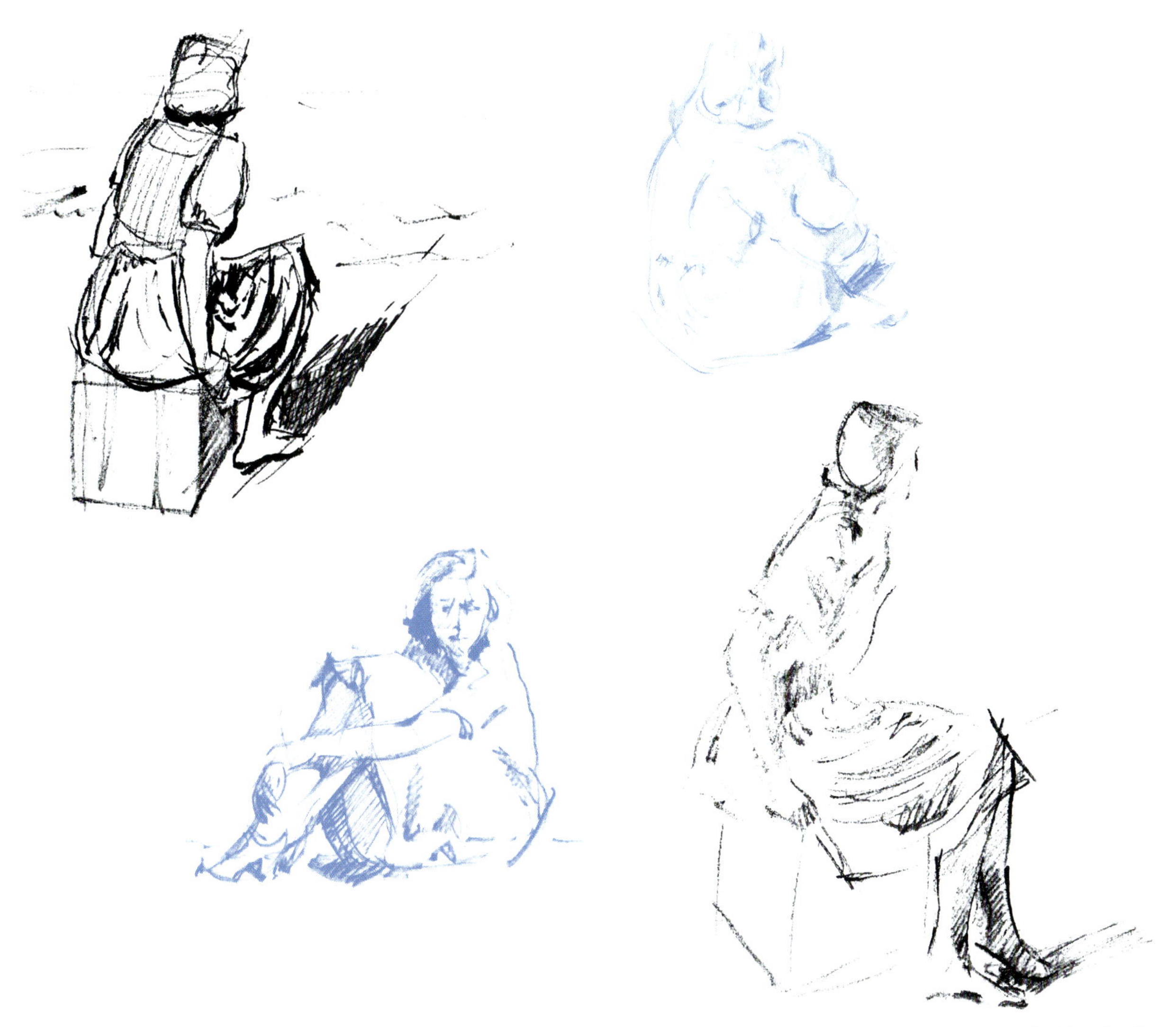

GIRL DRAWINGS
sketchbook drawings

The first "Girl on the Beach" picture Elden painted the summer of 1948 was "Water's Edge," an oil, 25 x 30 inches. At the Saturday morning Farnsworth criticism, Jerry looked at it for a long time and then said it "just missed being a very handsome picture" because the colors were too bright. However, it was accepted for the August exhibition at the Provincetown Art Association. It was also shown at The Sarasota Art Association Gallery Opening Exhibition February 1949. It was later destroyed.

Elden found a place in Hyannis where he could make frames until the Stanley Marsh miter box he ordered arrived, and added to our income by making frames for the Farnsworth students. He also joined the new Cape Cod Art Association in Hyannis.

"White Gulls Flying," the second large "Girl on the Beach" painting had a story that was enough to gladden the heart of any struggling young artist—and his wife. The figure of a girl in a timeless costume sitting on a box gazing out into a misty, moody vastness where land meets the sea.. It was

hung in the Cape Cod Art Association show and was seen by Dr. and Mrs. Thron. A day later they came back to buy it, only to find that the gallery was closed. The owner of the sporting goods store next door went all the way across town to get the key and made the $500 sale. Ironically, the reason the gallery wasn't open was that it was Elden's turn to gallery sit and he and Eleanor Hodgins had taken off following a report of a beached whale in East Dennis. In another strange twist in the story of "White Gulls,"—a few days later a chaffeur-driven station wagon appeared at the trailer with another prospective buyer wanting that same painting!

Dr. Thron's letter after the painting was shipped to him in New Jersey says, "The painting expresses to all of us some of the indescribable attraction of The Cape, which we have long felt."

Eleanor and Eric Hodgins and little Patty graciously accepted our invitation for a celebratory lobster dinner in Hyannis, and we discovered that Eleanor and I shared the same birthday—September 24th!

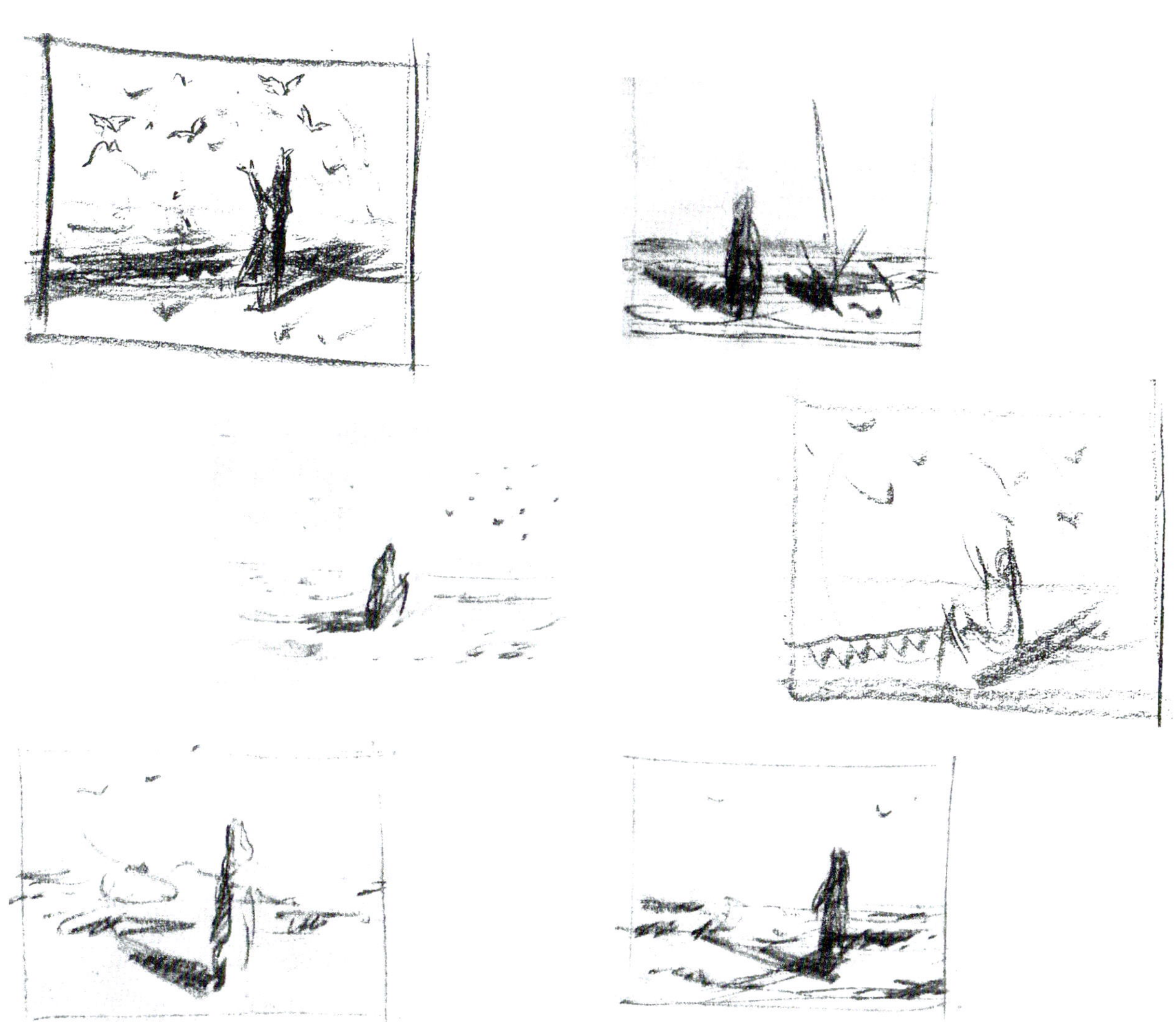

GIRL DRAWINGS
sketchbook drawings
"White Gulls Flying"

With one exception, the "Girl on the Beach" figures were painted in the loft of Mr. Howes' barn. The exception was "Blue Water." For that one, I sat on the rough surface of a big rock with the cold waters of Cape Cod Bay splashing up around me. Elden and I would go lurching down the beach until we got to the rocky area, carrying palette and easel and big box of oils and, more often than not, with the brisk breeze catching the 28 x 36 canvas like a sail. Elden considered "Blue Water" was not a success because it lacked his imaginative background.

The figure for another large "Girl on the Beach" painting was completed in Mr. Howes' barn. Journal entry for August 26, 1948, reads: "I was standing with a blindfold around my eyes and my hands extended as if groping to find what is ahead. It was quite tiring and very boring and I'm sure I was a horrible model. I couldn't hold the hands still so we propped them up with sticks." The title "Land's End" was probably inspired by the curved tip of Cape Cod, out beyond Provincetown. Elden could not arrive at a background that he liked, so the painting was taken to Sarasota in its unfinished state.

The first of September meant the time had come to wind things up and get ready to make the trip to Florida although many things made The Cape seem attractive then. We were excited to see a whale cruising around in the Bay processing sustenance through his huge wide open jaws. An especially brilliant display of aurora borealis lit up the whole sky like fireworks. The cranberry bogs were full of men (including Mr. Howes) rocking the bright red fruits in their scoops.

We spent some time looking at property, thinking of buying or building a home, perhaps at one of the lovely inland lakes, where "a very nice new two-bedroom house on a good sized lot on the water's edge" could be had for $6,000. However, we realized how short the season was on Cape Cod. So, once again, we started trailer traveling on my birthday, headed this time for Gettysburg, Pennsylvania.

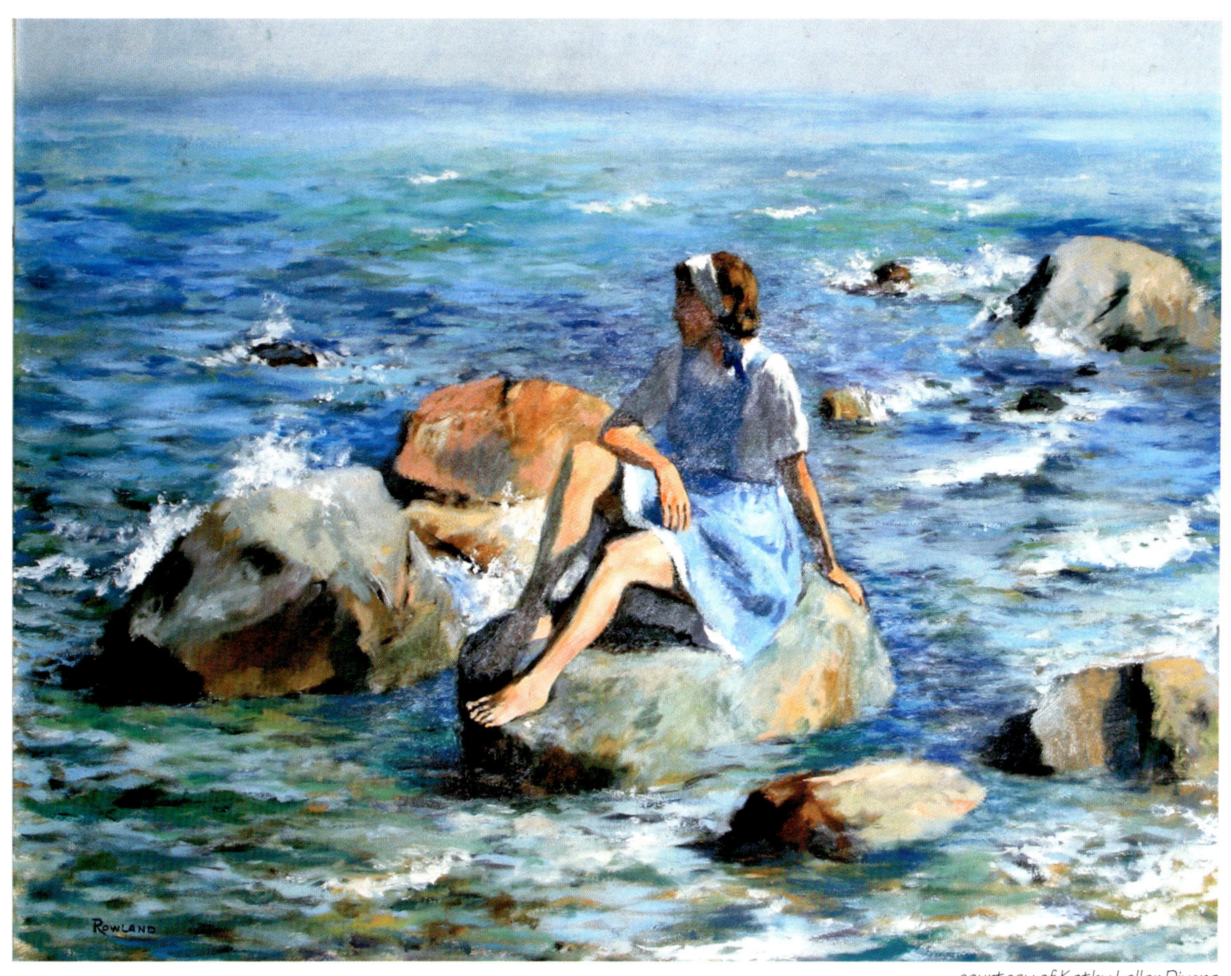

BLUE WATER
oil 1948
28x36

Eric Hodgins was going back to New York to work until Christmas. He drove Eleanor and Patty as far as Gettysburg where we met them to drive tandem with them to Florida. I rode in the Hodgins family's new Ford with Eleanor and Patty and Elden drove our car and trailer. All of us got together for nights at motels.

Before we left East Dennis that late September of 1948, it had been arranged that Elden would serve as monitor at the Farnsworth School in Sarasota that winter and I would again work as secretary to Mr. Caples.

In Sarasota, we parked our trailer at Ashby Court on the north side of town to be near the Farnsworth Studio at the airport. With gas at 26 cents a gallon (it had been 23 on The Cape) we felt a need to conserve. Mr. Caples arrived in late October but never was able to climb the steps to his office. So my duties were a kind of "curb service," involving my dashing down in response to Mose's sounding of the horn to talk to Mr. C. at the car, or going to see him at his favorite haunts across Lower Main Street.

Elden and I had decided it was time for us to have a place to live that was not on wheels. We spent every spare moment looking at lots, and at houses—to buy or to gather ideas. We poured over a Simon and Schuster book *Tomorrow's House, a complete guide for the home builder.* Published in 1945, it had exciting ideas for the "modern" house we wanted ours to be. Elden put our ideas together and made a complete set of scale drawings.

We found land on which to build our house: 100 feet facing a sand track three blocks from the Gulf of Mexico on Siesta Key. For $750 we bought two 50-foot lots in what had been developed in the 1920s as Sarasota Beach. It was on "a ridge," inches, maybe a foot, higher than its neighbors. Real estate agent Bea Brausa, mother of one of the models Elden had secured for the Farnsworth School, had a plat showing lines of these higher lands, remnants of age-old dune lines. It had attractive clumps of palms and two pine trees, unusual on The Key. The "Shell Gatherer" is at nearby Point-of-Rocks, a landmark by which boats could steer, and a favorite spot to watch sunsets.

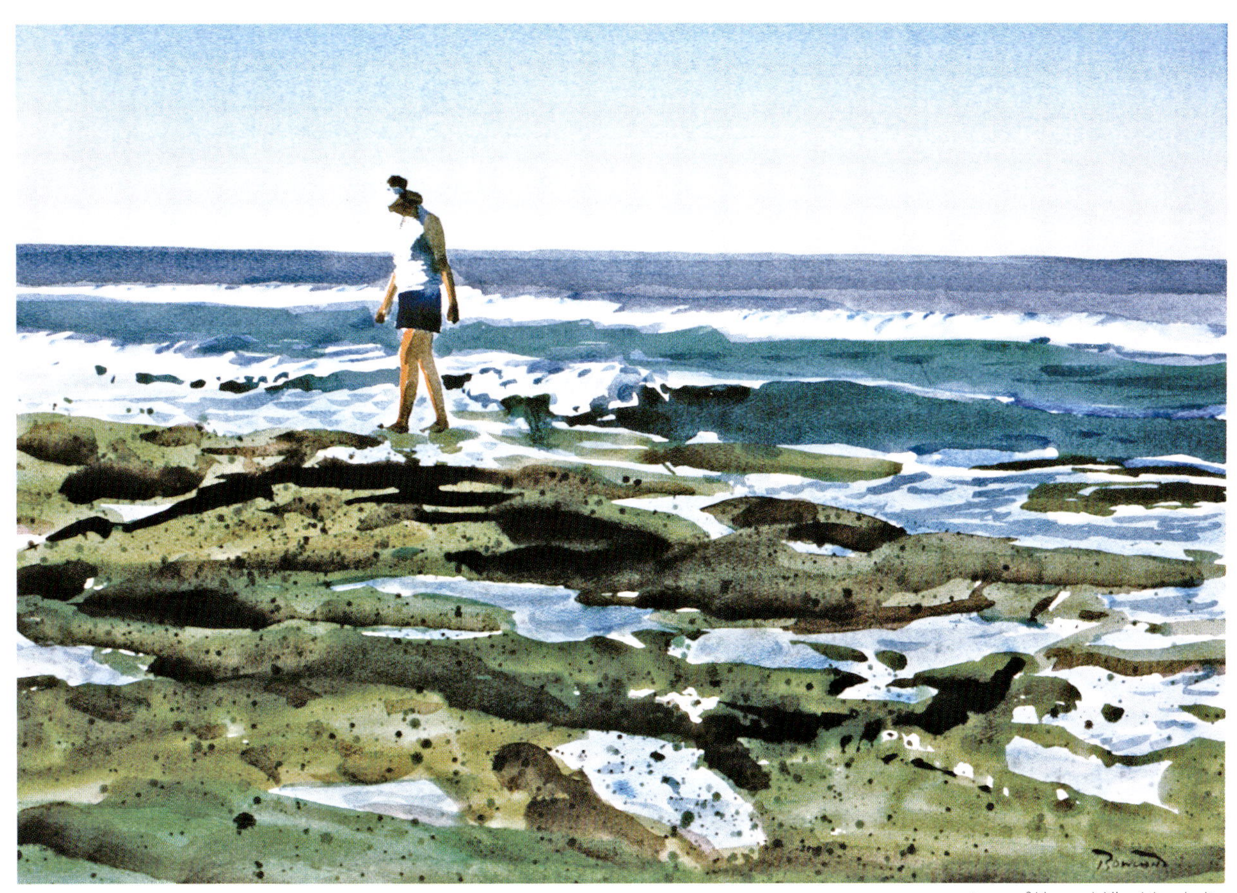

courtesy of Nancy Miller Myerholtz

SHELL GATHERER
watercolor
24x18

In the first days of November, 1948, scrub was cleared from our lot on Siesta Key preparatory to building our house. Elden had taken the plans and a sketch to an architect, and to Frank Archibald, original owner of the lot, but we decided to work with Harold Pickett, a designer with innovative ideas about how to build a unique house for a low cost. It was to be 24 x 28 feet, flat roof, with a four-foot overhang, lots of glass, with the corner toward the street to give it individuality, and to take advantage of a graceful clump of large palms in the middle of the lot. This left space for a studio building at the back of the lot and a hoped-for addition to the house on the street side. After a couple of years we were to learn that the name of the street was Avenida del Mare, having been named in the 1920s when Florida was fixated on the Spanish.

Work was started promptly by a couple of Florida old-timers who delighted in telling us that a hurricane would come and completely inundate the whole of Siesta Key. Elden stayed around, helping wherever he could, but also observing, and learning.

He also watched the erection of a new Sarasota Art Association building downtown in the Civic Center where they had been given the privilege of building a fine new gallery on city of Sarasota land.

Eleanor Hodgins had been most helpful in all of our house adventure. She also invited Elden to work in an apartment that she had rented as a studio and office at their home in McClellan Park. This allowed him to go back to the unfinished painting of the blindfolded girl, which he had brought from The Cape. After a struggle, he arrived at a moody background with a tropical theme. In the next two years, the finished painting was shown at the State Teachers College, Indiana, Pennsylvania, in his one-man shows in Tampa and Sarasota, and at the Delgado Museum, New Orleans. In New Orleans, it tied with another painting for the popular prize and the money was divided equally.

Sometime after March 11, 1951, when a photo of it appeared in the *Tampa Sunday Tribune*, Elden cut the painting down, leaving only the figure and a couple of Florida shells.

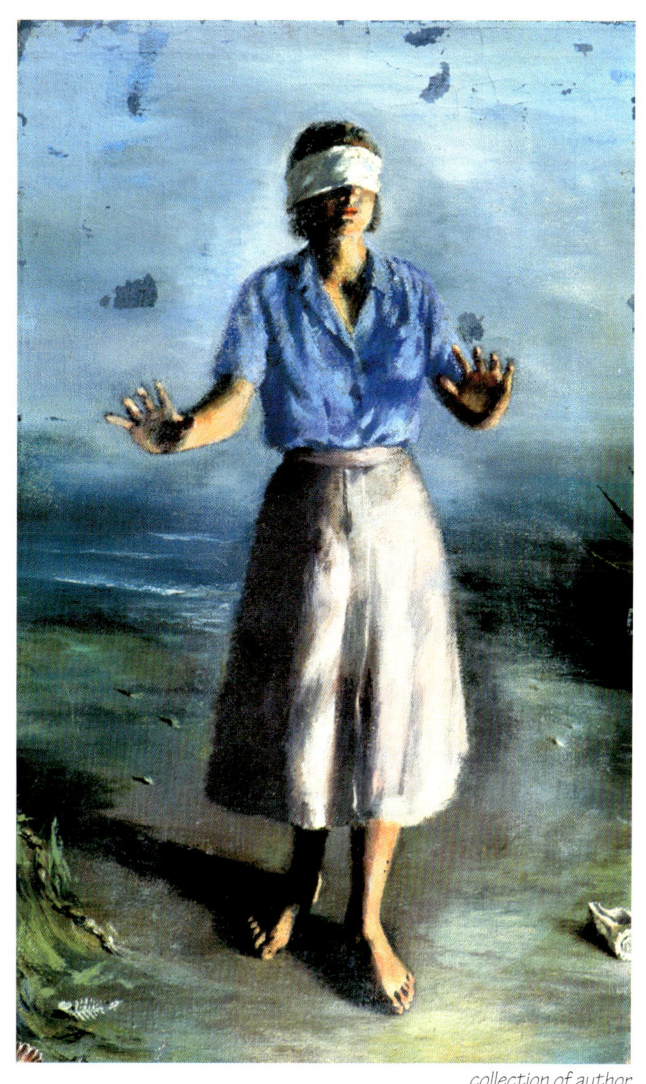

BLINDFOLDED GIRL
oil 1948
16x26

Work on our new house moved steadily along during the winter of 1948-49, but with some interruption for Christmas. In spite of his ill health, Mr. Caples made plans to send every minister in Sarasota a Christmas turkey and box of candy. Elden and I drove all over town making deliveries. I wrapped countless 3-pound boxes of candy, including one for myself.

Elden stained the pecky cypress board and batten exterior of the house a silvery gray. The timbers for the open beam ceiling were also to be stained gray. On New Year's Day, I was high on a ladder with my hands full of stain-soaked rags when a stream of visitors began to arrive. It turned out that our designer Harold Pickett had attended a New Year's Eve party at The Florida Art Colony Furniture Enterprise, which was being started by artist Syd Solomon, and the word got around about Pickett's exciting new ideas. Among those whom Syd brought were Hilton and Dorothy Leech, both well-known artists, who had the Amagansett Art School in Sarasota. In the following years, the Leeches were to be an important part of the Rowlands' life.

Elden and I moved into our new home on Siesta Key on January 27, just ten weeks after it was started. Our dining table was the top of the tabletop saw left behind by the carpenters, but we didn't mind that, because Elden could use it to make furniture for us. Eleanor Hodgins had a nurseryman completely fill the adobe-brick planter which enclosed the front corner of the house. For Christmas, The Farnsworth had given us a set of Stangl dinnerware. We were thrilled with the way the New Jersey pottery with a four-fruit theme carried out the hand-crafted quality of our new home.

Now we could have our white and yellow kitten, Bozo, come to live with us. The first time we had gone to the Picketts' home to talk about the design for our house, their cat had a litter of kittens and we immediately chose one, which had been growing as the house grew. Elden made many sketches of Bozo and, later, of our Siamese, Smokey. Meanwhile, Pickett Construction was working on a studio for the Farnsworth Art School on Higel Avenue, Siesta Key.

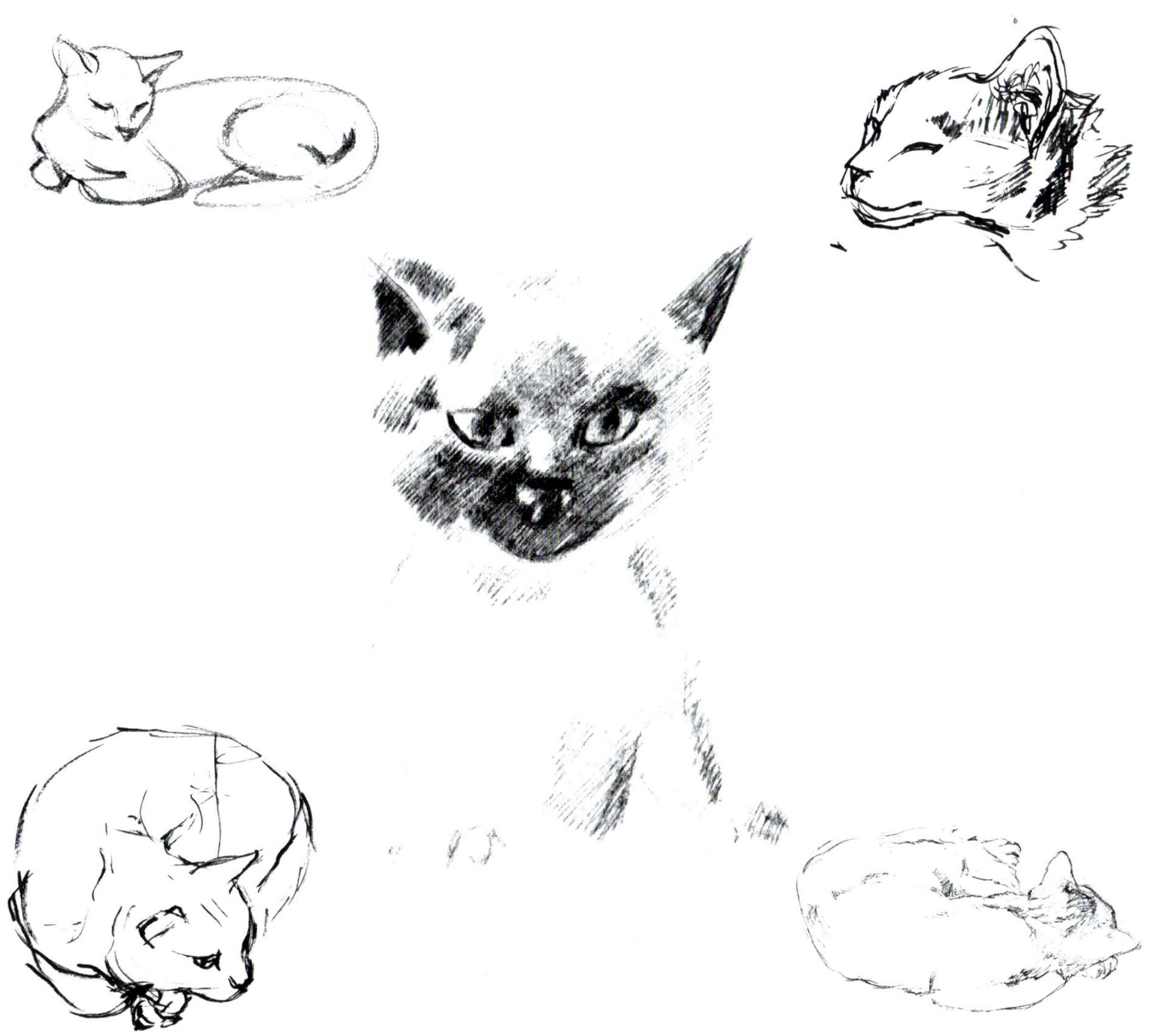

collection of author

CATS
sketchbook drawings

The new Sarasota Art Association Gallery opened on January 30, 1949. Over 1500 people attended the gala first opening. Elden and I sat with Patty Hodgins while her parents went to the opening and after they came home we went. Elden's painting "Water's Edge," the "Girl on the Beach" painting we had done on Cape Cod the previous summer, was exhibited in the entrance display window.

My employer, Ralph Caples, died in February. At the funeral I sat with other members of the Caples employee "family,"—Lyla Dykes, his former secretary, the five black servants, and Charles Pickett, who handled Mr. Caples' business affairs. It was a memorable occasion, sitting in the patio of the lovely Caples home (later to become a part of New College). Afterwards, as best I could, I helped Mrs. Caples with acknowl-edgements for over 180 floral pieces, and stacks of telegrams and sympathy notes.

And life went on. Although the Caples office was being closed, chairs were brought in for us to watch the annual Sara de Sota Pageant Parades pass below us. In the

afternoon, the children were charming and cute in their fanciful costumes and miniature floats. At night, a veritable Circus Extravaganza unfolded the length of Main Street, complete with calliopes, and clowns, and circus wagons bearing tigers and lions, and show girls riding elephants.

The fact that Ringling Brothers and Barnum and Bailey Circus wintered in Sarasota was central to the art community. Art classes, and individuals, spent countless hours sketching at the Circus Quarters. Elden's favorite subject was the statuesque show girls. In March, a clown and his little dog entertained at the opening of a show of circus subjects at the Art Association. Marion Cristiani was only one of the prominent artists who disappeared from the art scene when the Circus went on the road.

Elden and a group of students had fellow artist Margaret Sturgis pose outside of the regular Farnsworth portrait classes. Elden's small canvas (20 x 24) became one of the "Girl on the Beach" series, and was hung at the Sarasota Art Association Members' Show.

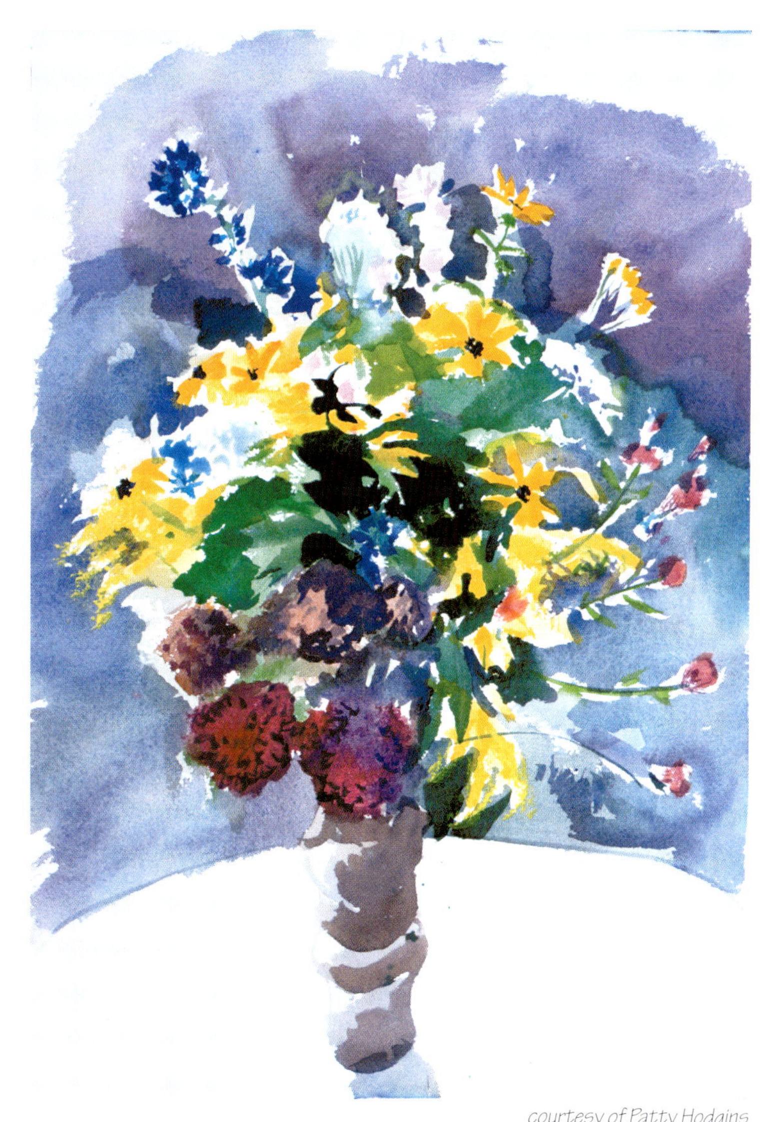

courtesy of Patty Hodgins

VASE OF FLOWERS
watercolor 1980

Elden and I went to Clearwater to see an exhibition at the Clearwter Art Museum in which his painting "Margaret" was included and had won the popular prize. Our favorite way to get from Sarasota to Clearwater was to take the car ferry across Lower Tampa Bay. The 7-mile trip from Piney Point in Manatee County to the southernmost tip of St. Petersburg in Pinellas County was a little bit of going to sea. It was possible to see ocean-going freighters out of the Port of Tampa and fun to watch the porpoises gracefully playing in our wake.

One night late in March the jungle behind our house caught fire! The 150-acre tract of native palmetto and waxy myrtle stretched more than half a mile with nothing to stop a fire between us and Midnight Pass Road. Elden and neighbors and volunteers worked frantically to cut a firebreak. By 11 o'clock the last recourse seemed to be retreating to the roof of the house with the garden hose—a great vantage point to see the cabbage palms go up like giant torches. Eventually, the fire burned itself out and we were left with the sight, and overpowering smell, of acres of blackened debris. We

were to learn that this burn-off occurred every two or three years in the dry late spring months. Also, we learned that Florida scrub restored itself in the heavy rains of summer, that the palm trees simply put out big new fronds from the center of the "cabbage," with only the blackened trunks to tell the tale.

An enthusiastic volunteer at the Art Association, Elden was elected to the Board to be chairman of the Exhibition Committee to schedule exhibitions, get juries, and install shows, a position he was to hold for many years. I, although not a dues-paying-member of SAA, suddenly found myself drafted to the Board as Secretary. Jerry Farnsworth had been head of the Nominating Committee and the word "Secretary" to him simply meant Katherine Rowland, willy-nilly.

The new Farnsworth School Building on Siesta Key opened with a festive dinner party around April 1. John Higgs, a student, had Harold Pickett build a house for him next door. Many of the students followed the Farnsworths to Cape Cod.

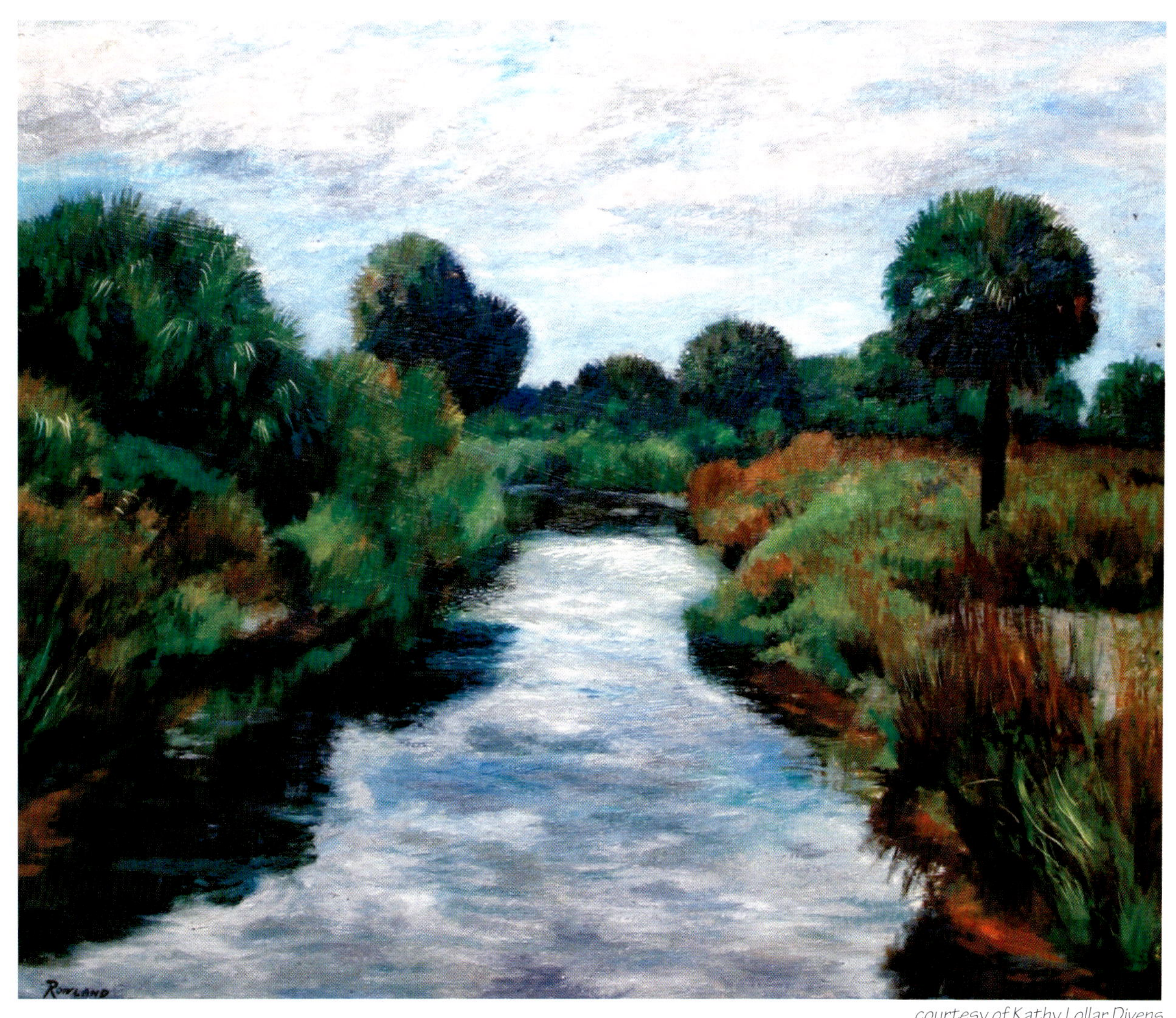

courtesy of Kathy Lollar Divens

DRAINAGE DITCH
oil 1950
24x20

The Rowlands had a very full time after the new Farnsworth Studio closed in the spring of 1949. I stayed with Patty Hodgins while Eleanor went to New York for two weeks. Elden came to enjoy the delicious dinners Hattie Davis, the maid, prepared every night. I posed for a "Girl on the Beach" figure, but he didn't have time to complete the moody background.

We planted a gardenia bush to celebrate our 10th wedding anniversary. We drove to Ohio to see friends and family and bring back some of our possession to use in our new home. I sewed dozens of yards of 54-inch unbleached muslin into panels to be hung on traverse rods over the 32 feet of glass in the living room—since there were no neighbors around, privacy was not important, but keeping out the glare of the sun was. Through it all we rescued our young cat, Bozo, who found endless ways of getting himself into trouble in the jungle around the house.

We rented the house for the summer to Margaret Miller, an artist friend who was director of the Tampa Art Institute.

On June 12th we retrieved our trailer from the Ringling students to whom we had rented it at Ashby Court and started on our way to Cape Cod, taking Bozo along, thereby enlivening the trip considerably.

The Hodgins family had rented a house in Truro that summer. We settled our trailer in Brownie's Piney Woods Camp outside Wellfleet, where we had spent our first night on Cape Cod in 1946. Elden found space to work in the loft of Florence Rich's Gallery in the center of the little town of Wellfleet. He painted in the moody background of the 28x36 oil we had started in Sarasota, and titled it "Silent Hour 2." The next year it was shown at Atlanta and at the Sarasota Art Association. It was purchased by Eleanor Friedman, a Sarasota sculptor who exhibited under the name of Hushi Garfield.

Elden made a tentative start on his Wellfleet art classes. The first student was Doris Campbell. A school teacher from the Boston area who spent summers on the Cape, she, Elden, and I, were close friends for years to come.

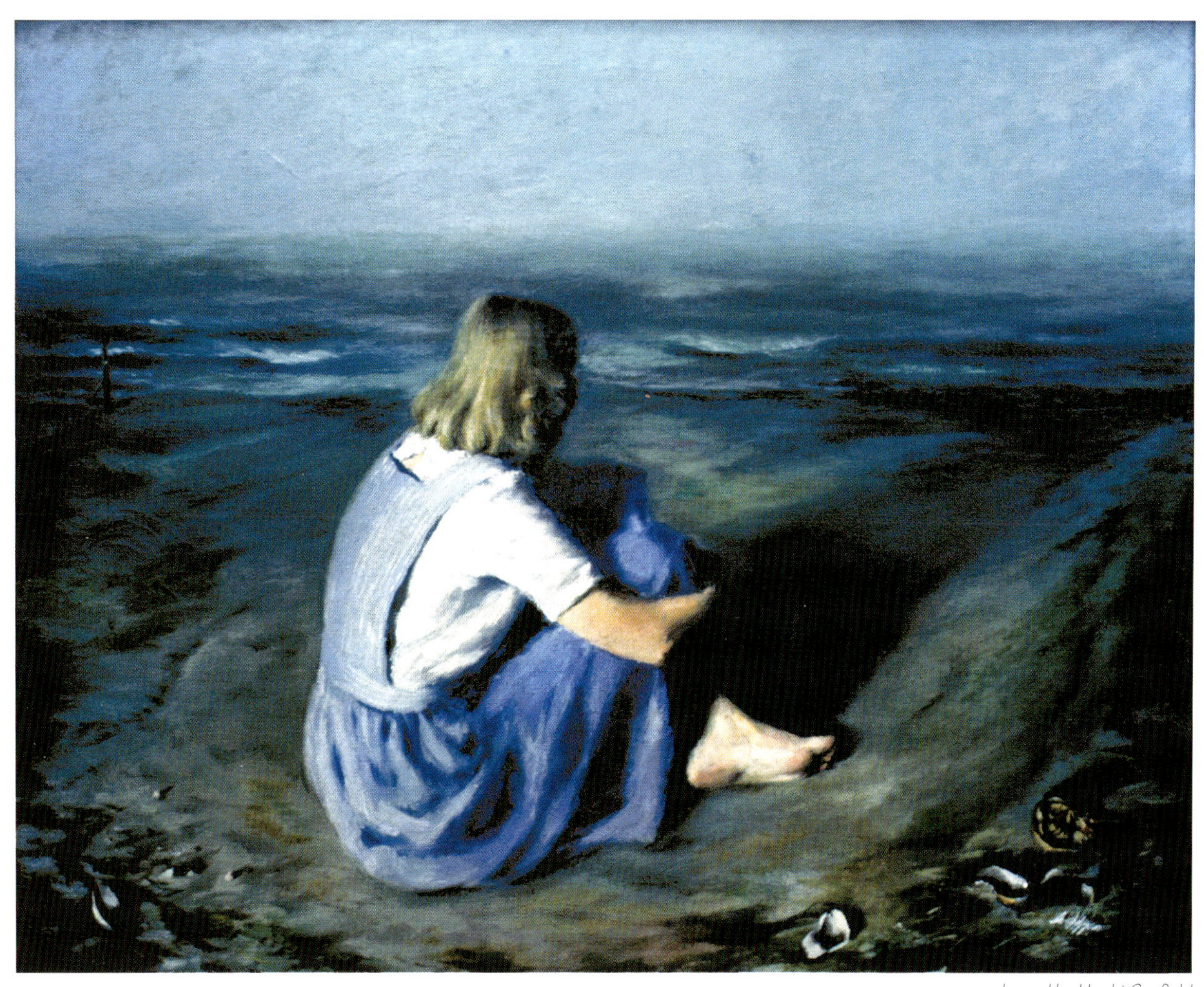

SILENT HOUR
oil 1949
28x36

The Covered Wagon trailer, our traveling home for four years, stayed behind under the fire tower at Wellfleet when Elden and I left for Florida the fall of 1949.

Back at Sarasota, Elden immediately began to build a studio for himself behind our house on Siesta Key. It was 16x20 feet, had a shed roof, with high windows the length of the north side, in approved studio fashion, with small shower room and counter kitchen along one end. There was an 8-foot deck on the sunny south side. Like the house, it was pecky cypress, board and batten, stained gray. Except for contracting out the concrete slab, electrical work and plumbing, Elden did it all himself, thanks to his experience remodeling our first trailer in 1945.

The house had been finished in January for $6,450, including the lots. The studio, completed in December, cost $1800. The first year's property tax bill for the land and two buildings was $22.57.

 I went to work in Sarasota City Hall, which over-arched Lower Main Street leading out onto The Pier. Charles Pickett, the City Treasurer, having known me at Mr. Caples' office, found a place for me in the Tax Department. Tax bills were figured and printed on a computer-forerunner, a huge, clattering monster that caused me great distress every time I missed as much as a single keystroke. However, I learned to work with property records and maps, a skill that I was later to enjoy doing genealogy research.

The Sarasota Art Association added The Patio Gallery that summer. An addition to their original building in the Civic Center, it consisted of four covered galleries in a square, around an open-roofed, open-walled patio. For the first show in the enlarged gallery space, six artists were invited for a group of one-man shows: Robert Chase, Shirley Clement, Roger Holt, Jack Newberry, Elden Rowland and Lois Bartlett Tracy. The show opened the night of November 26, 1949, to near-freezing temperatures. Elden's work was shown on one of the patio walls. It was a happy occasion, in spite of the fact that the cold weather meant the new dress I had made especially for that event had to be covered with a winter coat!

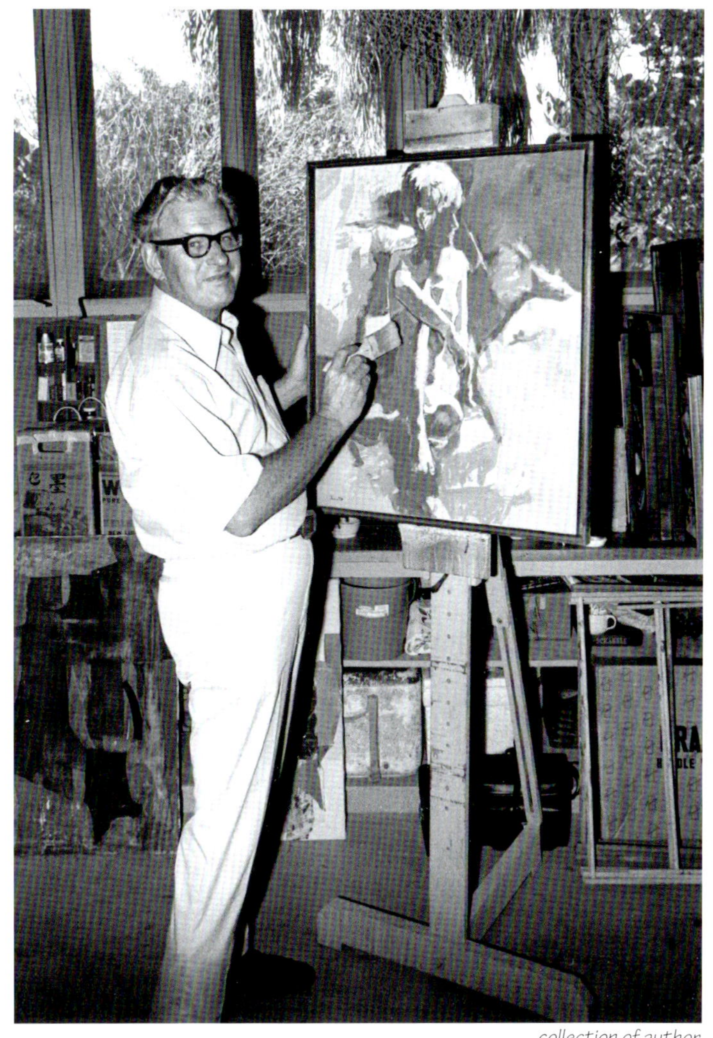

collection of author

IN THE STUDIO
photograph of artist
5x7 b/w

Three of Elden's "Girl on the Beach" paintings were in the Sarasota Art Association's Patio Gallery show in the fall of 1950: "Girl With Dories," and "Land's End," and "Storm Coming."

 When the *Herald-Tribune* photographer asked the six artists to pose with their favorite paintings for a story in the November 26 newspaper, Elden chose "Girl with Dories." Two weeks later, he and "The Girl" appeared again because he gave that painting to the Art Association as a door prize in their Christmas show. Almost a thousand visitors registered during the two-week period. The winner was Robert Noedel, a student at the Ringling School of Art.

"Land's End," (also known as "Blindfolded Girl") was shown in its full 28x36 dimension, before it was cut down.

"Storm Coming" was shown, among other places, at the Art Association of Newport's (Rhode Island) 40th Annual Exhibition; also at Nieta Cole's Gallery in Orleans, Massachusetts. One of the amusing little glitches which happen in an artist's life occurred in connection with the latter show: The *Cape Cod Standard-Times* on Wednesday, Aug. 15, 1951, headlined "Howland Show is Opened," and went on talking about "Mr. Howland" well into the article before they realized this was not one of the historic Cape Cod families, whose names often appeared in their weekly news sheet.

The Art Association's fine new galleries were an indicator of the flowering in the Sarasota art community that was to come in the Fifties and Sixties decades. The visual arts led the way. Formed in 1926 by a group headed by Marcia Rader, supervisor of art in the county school system, the Art Association was given impetus around 1930 when nationally-known artists, such as George Pearse Ennis and Hilton Leech, came to town to help start the Ringling School of Art. The Reverend Glen Tilly Morse helped keep it alive during the years of World War II. Helen Sawyer and Jerry Farnsworth came and attracted adult students who established homes and were supportive of other arts, including The Players and the newly-forming West Coast Symphony.

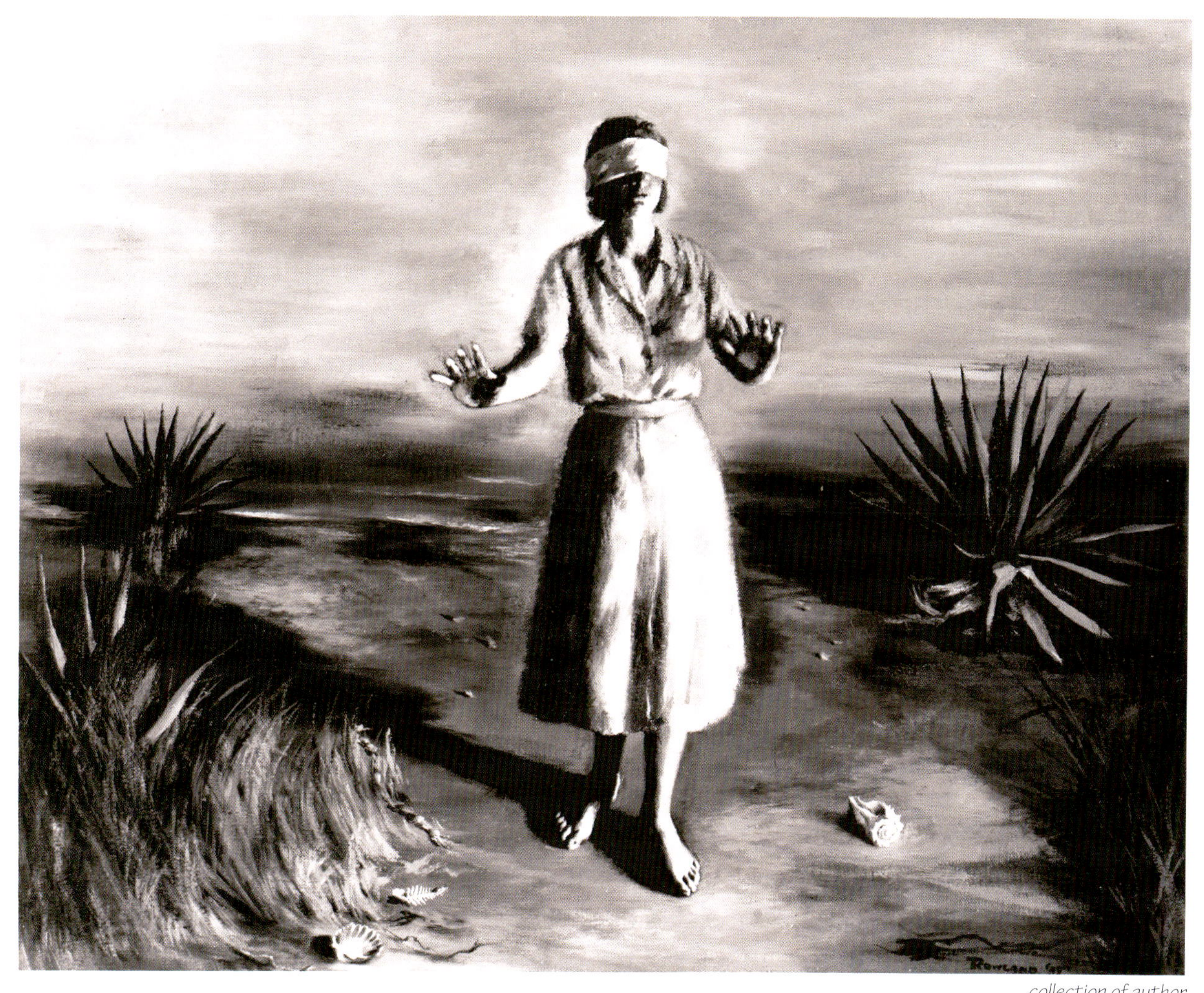

LAND'S END
oil 1948
28x36

The story of organizations and art schools that were part of the dynamic growth in the Sarasota art community in the 1950s is well told in *A History of Visual Art in Sarasota,* written by Pat Ringling Buck, Marcia Corbino and Kevin Dean, and published by University Press of Florida in 2003. The Rowlands became a part of that scene in the winters and continued to go to Cape Cod during the summers.

The small oysterman's town of Wellfleet, on Cape Cod, became "our town" for the summers through 1955. Elden rented the old blacksmith shop for his painting classes. The first year, it had a dirt floor and the old forge still in place. After that, a concrete floor was poured and the forge taken out, freeing room in which Elden built a compact cabinet for my "art materials store." The only source for art materials nearer than Provincetown, 12 miles away, it was a blessing for students and the many professional artists of Wellfleet, as well. In addition, I was able to use my knowledge of materials learned while working at Barry's in Sarasota the winter before.

Located near the Town Pump, the studio was on Commercial Street, on the way to Wellfleet Harbor. The large double doors always stood open and admitted an interesting flow of visitors—from Xavier Gonzales and his wife, Edward Edwards, renowned artists who had their school just up the street, to dogs, and cats, and an occasional chicken. Not all the native Cape Codders were happy about the influx of artists, resulting, once in a while, in small boys riding by on their bicycles shouting "summer complaint." In the midst of all of this, Elden had active classes, with portrait models in the morning, landscape and still life after lunch.

Having sold our trailer, we started renting a series of cottages. The first was one of two set cozily side by side called "Priscilla" and "John Alden." Ours was John Alden. It was typical picturesque Cape Cod inexpensive rental of the time: silvery gray shingles, indoor bathroom but no hot water. The two-burner kerosene stove took far too long to heat water enough to boil the delicious fresh lobster from Eddie Dickey's pound down the road.

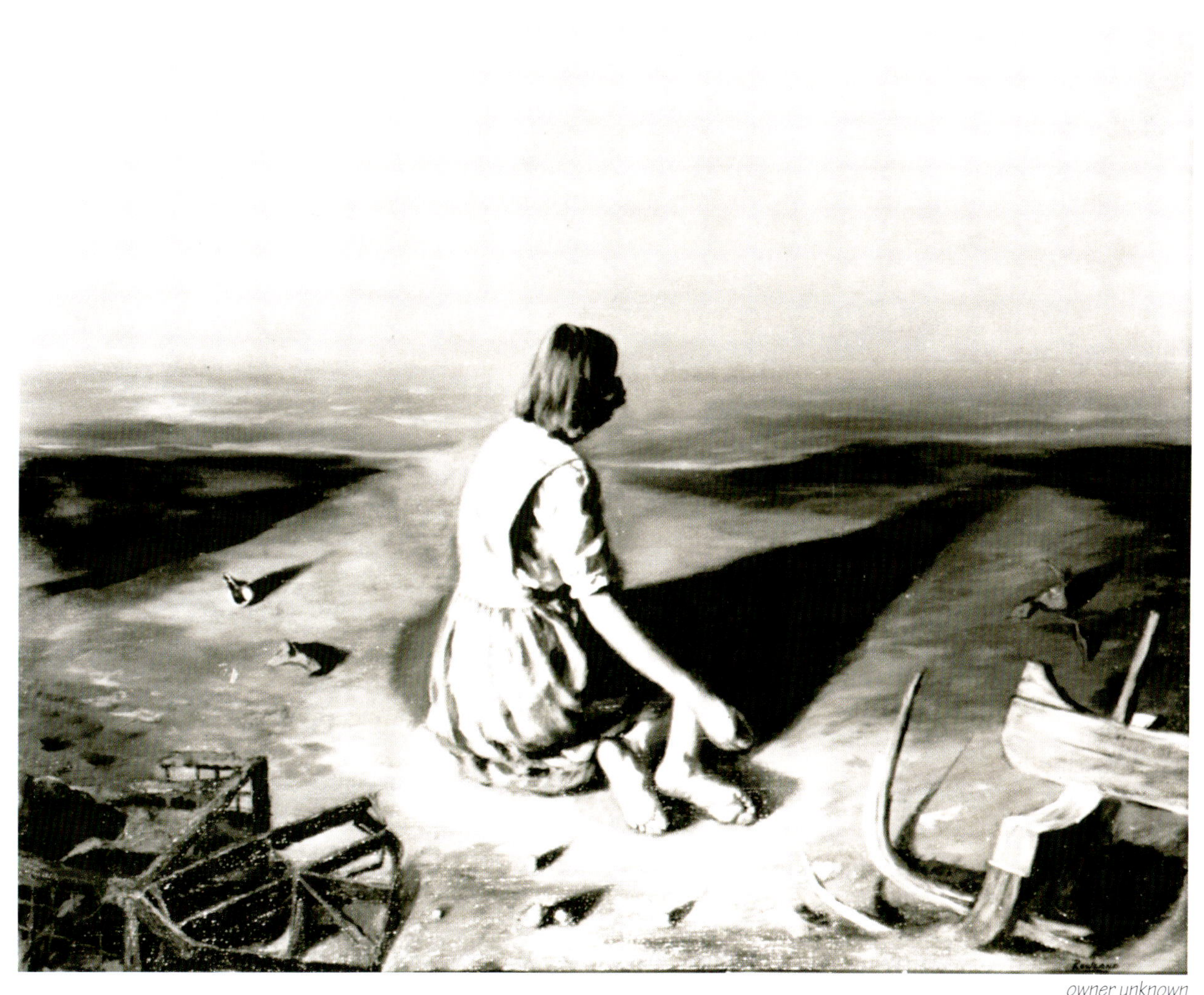

DAY AFTER TOMORROW
oil 1950
30x36

In the 1950s Elden began to teach in Sarasota in the winter, as well as having his painting classes on Cape Cod in the summer.

In 1952 he joined Laura E. Lock, a gifted, gracious lady of English descent, who was one of the pioneer artists of Sarasota. She had just built a new studio near the Bay front on Strawberry Avenue. She and Elden had a two-person show at the Art League of Manatee County in Bradenton that December.

Elden was one of the first teachers at the Manatee Art League, from the time it was located at the old Bradenton waterworks before the new galleries were built in 1956-57. He was on the board of directors and had worked on the planning of the new galleries with Janet Reid Kellogg, an accomplished artist, and Royal Kellogg, a retired lumberman, the driving forces of the new facility. For one of the opening exhibitions, Elden's work filled the Searle Gallery and that of Hilton and Dorothy Leech, the Kellogg Gallery.

Elden's teaching at the little fishing village of Cortez had a delicious side effect. We had let our place on Siesta Key to Edward Burlingame Hill, a distinguished member of the music community, and rented a house in Cortez for the winter. A typical old Florida style house—white frame, metal roof, up on blocks, screened porch on the front, it had room and quiet for Elden to paint. A couple of blocks away, Ellen and August Anttilla owned and operated the big old Albion Inn (later the Coast Guard Station). Ellen, who cooked wonderful meals for the guests, was also a painter, and she traded meals for Elden's art instruction—made us all happy!.

That winter I was setting up a book-keeping system for the Sarasota Art Association and often went to town early in the morning. Cortez Road, bordered by abandoned vegetable fields all the way to the Tamiami Trail, was a fairyland. Tall feathery grasses and overgrown flower stalks, each draped with dew-laden spiderwebs sparkling in the Florida sun, made a sight long to be remembered.

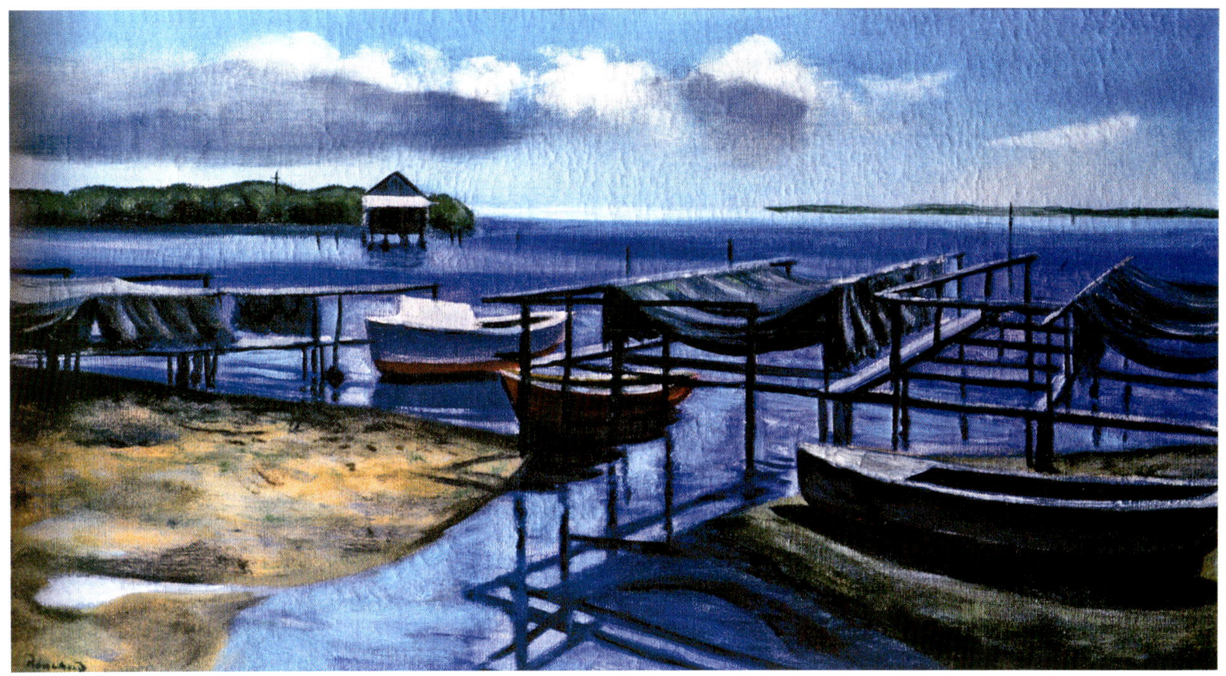

CORTEZ
oil 1956
40x20

In the first half of the 1950s Elden worked in traditional oil techniques. He did several in the "Girl on the Beach" series, painted still lifes and portraits, and studied the native Florida palmetto scrub. He also began to explore new media and ways of interpreting subject matter.

"Moss Country," of a darker mood than the other Girl paintings (perhaps I set the mood by wearing a moss green dress I had made) still won the popular prize at the Golden Anniversary Exhibition of the Delgado Museum in New Orleans. In his letter of notification, Director Alonzo Lansford said it: "received more than twice the number of votes; also, that he was surprised that so fine a painting had won a popular award." It received a Special Mention in the Atlanta Museum Southeastern Annual; and it was responsible for Elden's having a one-man show at the Tampa Art Institute when their Exhibition Chairman saw it at the Sarasota Art Association. It was purchased by the Rosensteins of Tulsa, Oklahoma, out of the Sarasota show.

Another "Girl on the Beach" painting was sold from a Sarasota show: "Communion," won a popular prize and was acquired by Mrs. Polly Wilson, the first time it was shown. Mrs. Wilson was a member of Sarasota social and civic circles whom I much admired. It pleased me that the figure made her think of her daughter, Paula.

"Day After Tomorrow" caused quite a lot of excitement in the Rowland family when we received a telegram saying it had won First Prize of $250 and the Richard Mitton Memorial Gold Medal at the exhibition of paintings by 100 Contemporary New England Artists sponsored by Jordan Marsh Company in Boston. Mr. Campbell, father of our friend Doris, represented Elden at the presentation, and, according to Rosemary Phelan, Director of the Exhibition, "thoroughly enjoyed himself." We thoroughly enjoyed seeing the photographs in the *Christian Science Monitor* and other papers. A review called "the painting of a girl sitting back-to on a beach a gem. The mood is haunting, the depth of composition unusual and the paintwork and drawing impeccable."

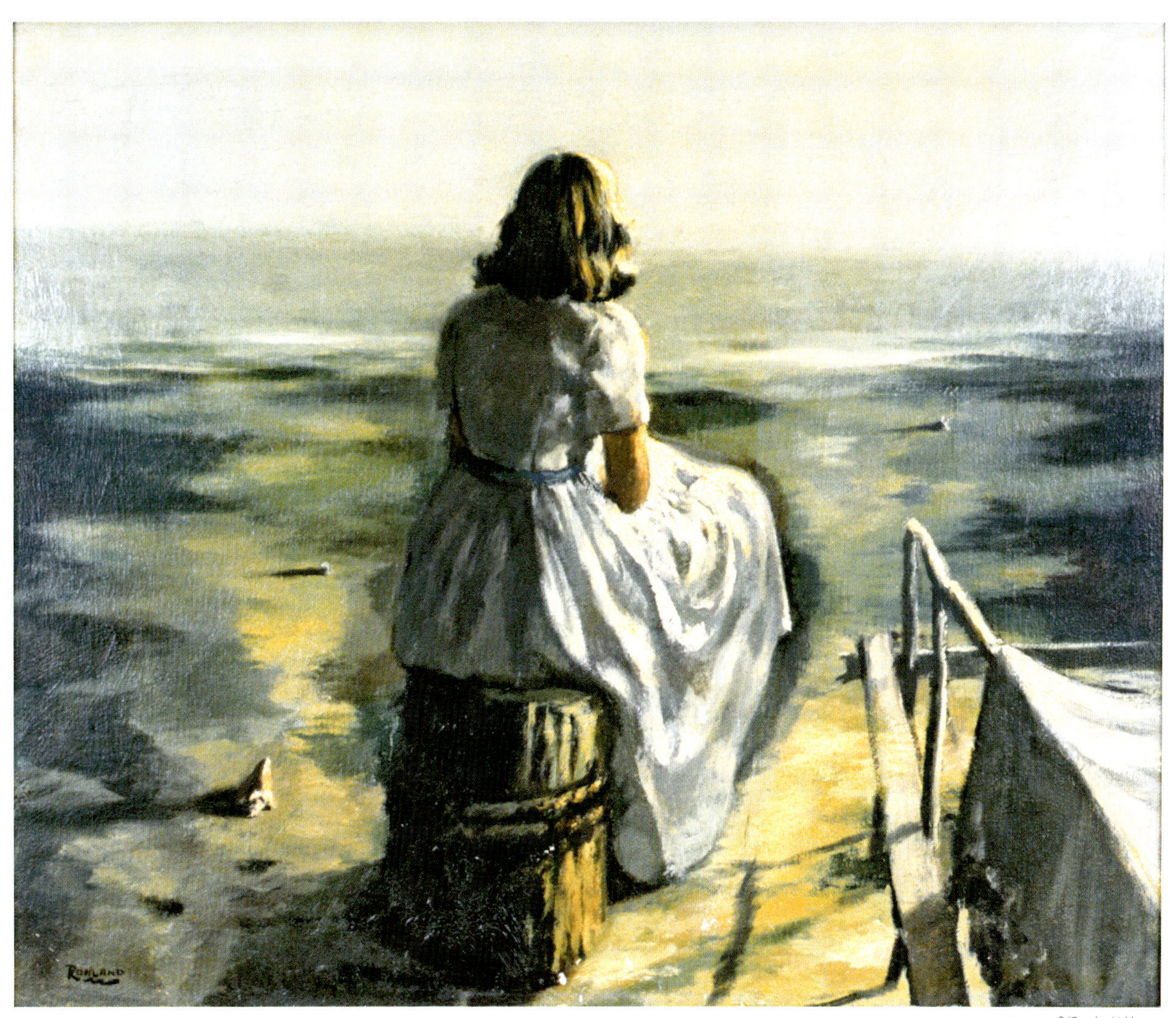

courtesy of Paula Wilson

COMMUNION
oil 1949
30x25

Elden had a good opportunity to indulge his eagerness to try new media in the summer of 1955 when he was commissioned by the Monsanto Company to do two works for their Plastics Division at Springfield, Massachusetts. Dr. C. Kilbourne Bump, Assistant Director of Research, who painted in Elden's class in Wellfleet, arranged for Elden to use a new product they were developing. Powdered color was added to a mixture of styrene plastic and mica and water to produce two large paintings:, a four foot by six foot triptych "Growth of Monsanto," and three by five panel, "Growth of Science (Ages of Man in Materials)." We signed in at the Indian Orchard plant to see them installed on June 16, 1955, the larger one over the stairway at the Research Lab and the other on the landing above.

Checks for $900 and $400 reached us when we were living in Cortez. Elden framed the checks and hung them over his worktable as a surprise for me (needless to say, we soon unframed them). Thirty years later, a letter from Dr. Bump told us the paintings were still in place, although he had retired by that time. The facility, now called Solutia, is the largest chemical manufacturing facility in New England.

Elden also used the Monsanto experimental product for several works that were exhibited in Florida. "Carnival," was hung in the Ringling Museum as part of the Sarasota Art Association's 1957 Circus Show. Review by Lawrence Dame in *The Herald-Tribune* describes it: "Flamboyant, puzzling to many, paint squeezed and slapped onto a panel, in lines and patches crisscrossed, with no definite image intended, . . make up an abstract impression of the blare and color of circus"—a clear indication that Elden was not only using an experimental medium but was exploring new treatment of subject matter, as well. Another, "Florida Power and Light," was shown in the SAA Explorations in Art Exhibition that same year and in his one-man show at Winter Haven.

Al Buell, a well-known illustrator, wanted to reconstruct a medium that Rubens had used and asked Elden to work with him, a short-lived, but interesting project.

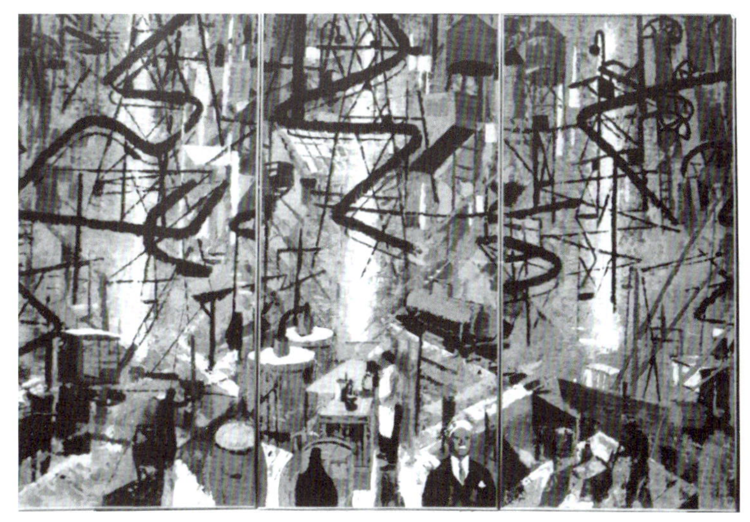

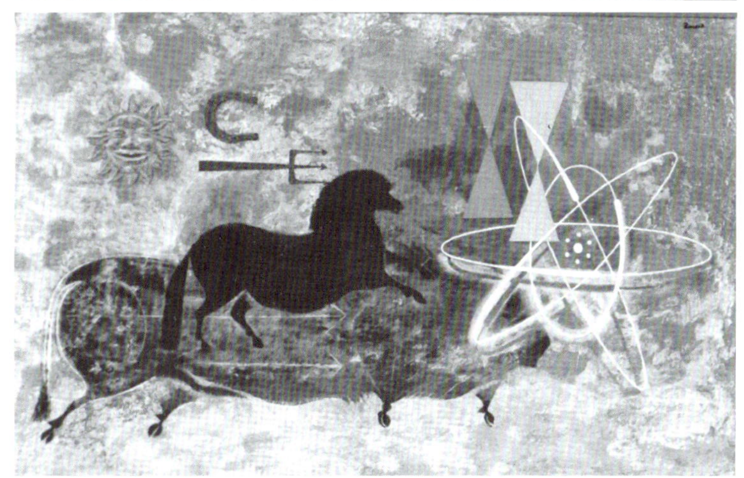

GROWTH OF MONSANTO
plastic 1955
48x72

GROWTH OF SCIENCE
plastic 1955
36x60

In the spring of 1956 Lawrence Dame did a series of interviews with artists. Elden's, done while we lived in Cortez, was headlined "Roving Artist Settles Here to Experiment." Although the accompanying photograph looked something like a mug shot, its cut line was pretty well on point:
"Ardent Quester in the art field is Elden Rowland, painter and teacher." Some excerpts from the text seem on point, too:
 Dame: "He's a tall, easy-smiling and drawlingly witty character who might well have come from rural spaces of Maine or Vermont instead of from Cincinnati with Kentucky mountain stock behind him. He has won many popular prizes, particularly with his noted 'girl on beach' pictures, and he can be slickly realistic or puzzlingly abstract as the spirit moves."

Rowland, talking about the Monsanto product: "I just patched the bathroom floor with it. It's great stuff."

"If I can not paint in about eight different styles, I'm not happy. Pictures aren't the end in themselves. They're a by-product of the artist's growth. They are the traces a man leaves behind of his thought and study."

In that period when abstract painting was just beginning to come to the fore, there were differences of opinions among the artists about the value of traditional and "modern" painting. During Elden's years as Exhibition Chairman of the Sarasota Art Association he was eager to have artists open to new things. He wrote a full column article which appeared Jan 6, 1957, in the *Herald-Tribune* headed, "Explorations in Art Tops SAA Exhibits." He outlined the history of the show starting with the rather tricky entries in the "Experimental Show." He ended by saying, "An exhibition such as this becomes an annual event only so long as it truly represents a spirit which is alive in the art community. . . It is my sincere hope in the years to come it will continue to grow, and to mirror the growth of our Florida artists in their search for what is beautiful and expressive."

In contrast, in an Sarasota Art Association demonstration of portrait painting "Five Artists and a Model," the artists were: Betty Warren Lancaster, Dorothy Sherman Leech, Jay Protas, Elden Rowland, and Loran Wilford.

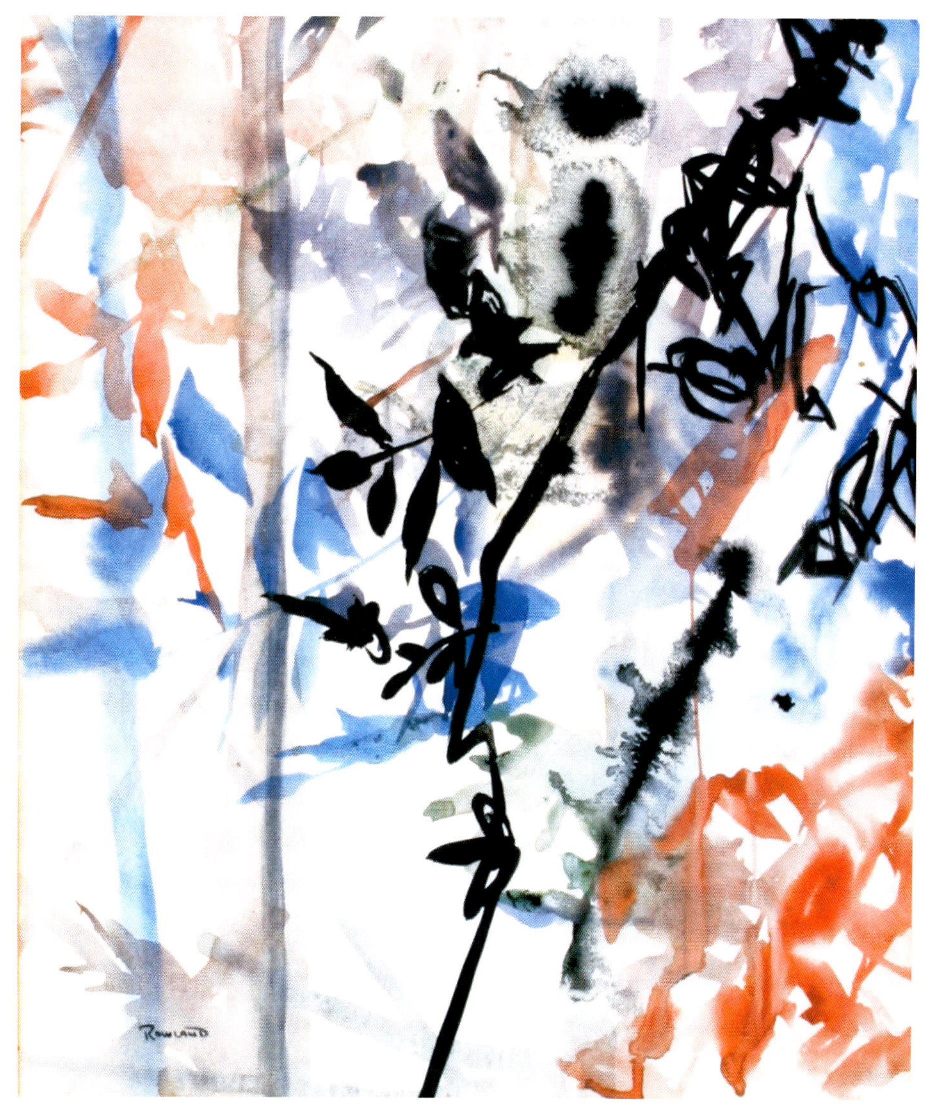

courtesy of Kathy Lollar Divens

LEAF SHADOWS
watercolor 1954
18x20

"Abstract Designs in Nature" was the title of a slide program developed by Elden and presented by him at many art organizations in the late 1950s. In a paragraph written to explain his rather obscure subject, he wrote: "The natural world will often reveal itself in surprising and intimate ways to the trained eye of the painter, who specializes in seeing. . . The color transparencies are not intended to justify abstract painting on the basis of occurrence of abstract designs in nature, but rather to point out that ordinary scenes can be seen in new ways, revealing unexpected beauty and suggesting mysteries for further exploration."

W. Clyde Burnett, art critic for the *Herald-Tribune*, after seeing the program, commented: "The slides were studied photographic abstractions from nature, as seen by the artist's eye. The pictorial variations were infinite, and the whole demonstration gave an insight into the artist's reaction to nature. . . Rowland is not a great talker, but he has a sure eye. His disciplined approach to his paintings is also evidenced through his photographic studies,

and thus it is evident that he has a sensitive vision. This being the case, the possibilities for his own growth and progression in painting are as infinite as his ability to continue to view nature."

Primarily, they were the awe-inspiring variety of ever-changing patterns of color and design revealed through the lens of his camera focused exactly on the surface of quiet water at fishing wharves in Cortez or The Pier at Bradenton. Later, Elden used nature patterns as inspiration for paintings, and taught a workshop "Nature, The Inexhaustible Source," with a similar theme.

Elden's propensity for experimenting, and his pleasure in working with wood, led him into making mobiles. Slim pieces of patiently sanded and polished pine or cypress, some as long as 6 or 8 feet, became perfectly balanced shapes of javelins, or sceptres, or wands. Suspended by invisible filament, the whole sculpture would turn effortlessly and fill the upper reaches of an entire room in an endlessly mesmerizing variation of pattern.

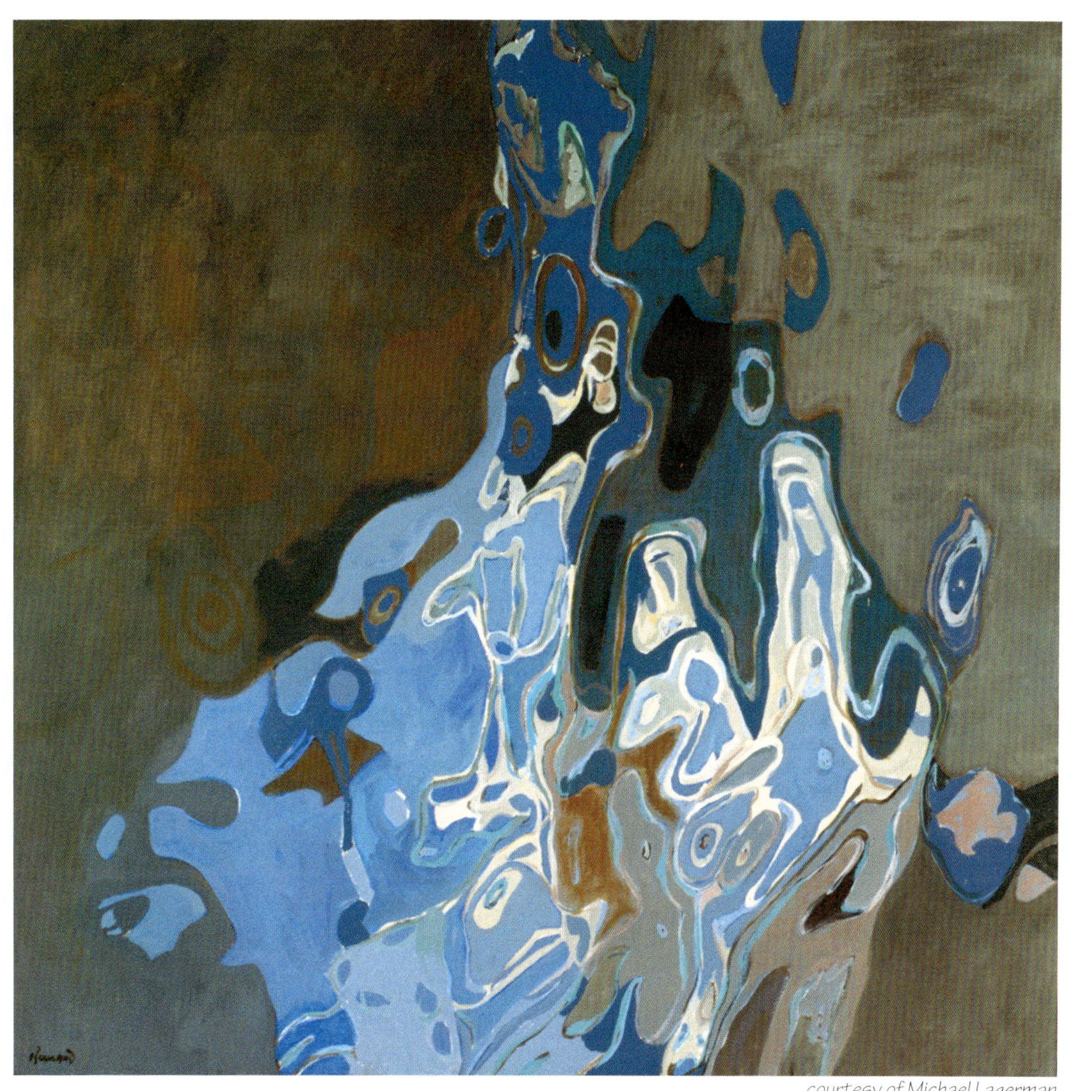

courtesy of Michael Lagerman

Arabesque
oil
35x36

One of Elden's long-armed mobiles won 2nd Award in the Sarasota Art Association's Sculpture and Ceramics Show in April, 1954. The letter informing Elden of the award carried the signature of Jack Cartlidge, co-chairman, with a tiny "kr" underneath. I had written the letter, as well as letters to all the other winners. It was my second season as person in charge at SAA. I had gone there the previous winter when Eleanor Treacy Hodgins became President, and remained when Stella C. Coler took the chair.

Elden did mobiles on different themes, as well. Reviewing the SAA Beachcomber Show, "S.H.F." said "'Fish Mobile' by Elden Rowland was amusing, but even more than amusing, it showed that the artist had studied his subject well. On close inspection the features of the fish which seemed to float in space were very able caricatures of tropical fish seen here. His spacing and construction were very good."

Certainly the ultimate in size and transitory appreciation of a mobile was one Elden constructed for the Beaux Arts Ball in

1955. Elden was asked to design and build the revolving structure to support cutout figures of eight super-sized dancing girls to whirl and twirl high in the Municipal Auditorium. Guy Saunders, and his students at the Ringling School, fashioned the figures. Elden supported the figures from tall stalks of giant bamboo to span the tremendous width of the dance floor, The flexibility of the live bamboo gave a springiness to the cut-outs as they revolved above the dancers.

Artists and art students spent much time and creative effort on costumes for the annual Ball. Prizes were highly coveted, Judy and Bill Axe winning the Most Beautiful category many different years. Elden and I never attended the Balls but that year we sat in the Spectators' Bleachers. Elden had an affinity with bamboo from his Oriental studies and expressed no doubt about his handiwork but I gave some thought to the fact that those gigantic spears could be lethal weapons should any supporting rope or knot fail. The next morning the huge pieces of bamboo became just one more pile of Florida's abundant yard trash.

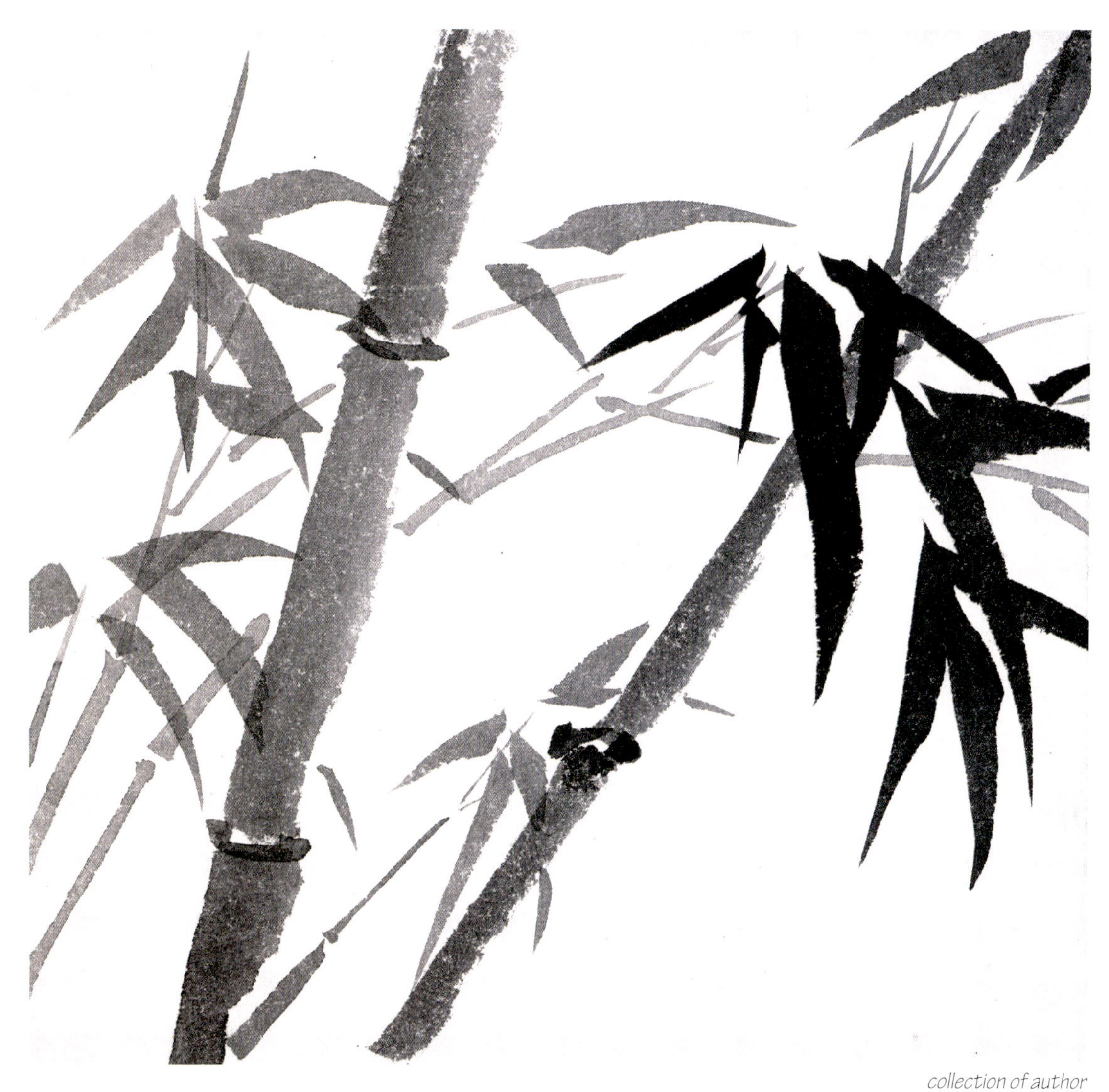

BAMBOO
sumi-e sketchbook
7³/₄ x 7

The Florida Artist Group, a new statewide non-profit organization was formed in 1949 of "practicing artists who had gained recognition nationally or statewide and whose work would contribute significantly to its exhibitions." Its stated purpose was the "stimulation of finer standards of the creative effort within the state of Florida." Elden was one of many Sarasota artists who were charter members. Thereafter, exhibitions and seminars were held in different cities each year.

Among leaders of the Florida Artist Group from the West Coast were Ralph H. McKelvey, Hilton Leech, and Helen Sawyer Farnsworth. "Headquarters" of FAG moved from time to time. For a number of years it was the Hartman Gallery in downtown Sarasota. In 1952, Martha and William Hartman, both painters, had rented part of an old newspaper building with space for large exhibitions, as well as their art school. They introduced many new Sarasota artists, invited the first group of women artists that became The Petticoat Painters, and staged the dramatic first showing of Ben Stahl's Stations of the Cross.

In 1952 Elden became volunteer circuit director of FAG at the request of Helen Sawyer, then the president. Later Elden handled circuit exhibitions for other statewide groups, Florida Federation of Art and Florida Craftsmen. In 1956 he formed his own Rowland Traveling Exhibitions. By January 1958 his bulletin listed 17 traveling art exhibitions.

He gathered works for themed exhibitions, secured bookings at art museums and associations, designed and printed catalogues, boxed, insured, and shipped the exhibitions by Railway Express. He handled it all himself, doing paperwork hunt and peck on a portable typewriter and reconciling his bank statements with an abacus. When the bank was slow in getting new blank checks to him, he made his own, and the bank honored them. His show, "Ruth White Printmakers" from a New York Gallery, was set on fire on the walls of a Georgia museum as a protest statement. On an occasion when we were driving our two loaded vehicles from Tampa, I looked in the rear view mirror of my car and saw a Sheriff's car ram into the side of his station wagon.

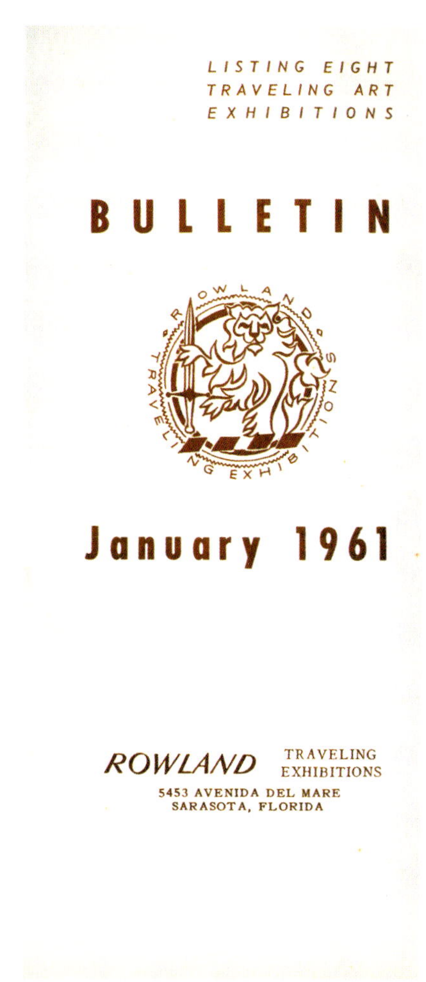

collection of author

TRAVELING EXHIBITIONS
bulletin 1961
4x9

Elden seldom sent his own paintings in his Traveling Exhibitions. Perhaps he felt reluctant to have them away for two years, as some artists did. However, over all, the response of artists and exhibitors was heart-warming. Correspondence with noted painter Byron Browne was so cordial and contained such beautiful calligraphy it is still a treasured memento. The gathering of paintings was an enjoyable way to meet new artists and see their studios. I sometimes went with Elden on The Cape and called at the artists' studios, often tucked away in the dunes or back street.

One amusing incident happened when we climbed the outside stairs of a silver-shingled building in Provincetown. At our knock on the door a voice said, "Enter." We entered and were greeted by a man seated behind a kitchen table, who seemed not at all taken aback by two strangers asking him to loan paintings. We had a very pleasant chat and he signed forms authorizing Elden to pick the paintings up at the Art Association, but we were puzzled why he did not go get the $3 or $4 cash for insurance.

Finally, with complete poise and dignity, he rose and went into the next room and come back with the money, not making the slightest reference to the fact he was wearing only boxer shorts, and no trousers. Nor did we.

Frank Crotty, an art reviewer for the Worcester (Mass.) Sunday *Telegram* became interested in the Traveling Exhibitions and wrote articles for his newspaper and the *Provincetown Advocate*. He devoted a chapter to Elden in his book *Provincetown Profiles* published in Barr, Massachusetts in 1958. Included were such other names as Edward Hopper, George Biddle, Xavier Gonzalez and Hans Hoffman.

Along with all his other activities, Elden continued with his own painting. The last "Girl on the Beach" for which I posed was "K. in Striped Dress," a 30 x 40 inch oil on canvas. He gave it to Maguire Hall of the Art Association of Richmond, Indiana. It is still in the permanent collection of the Richmond Art Museum, listed as "Communion," a duplication in name of an earlier one now owned by Paula Wilson.

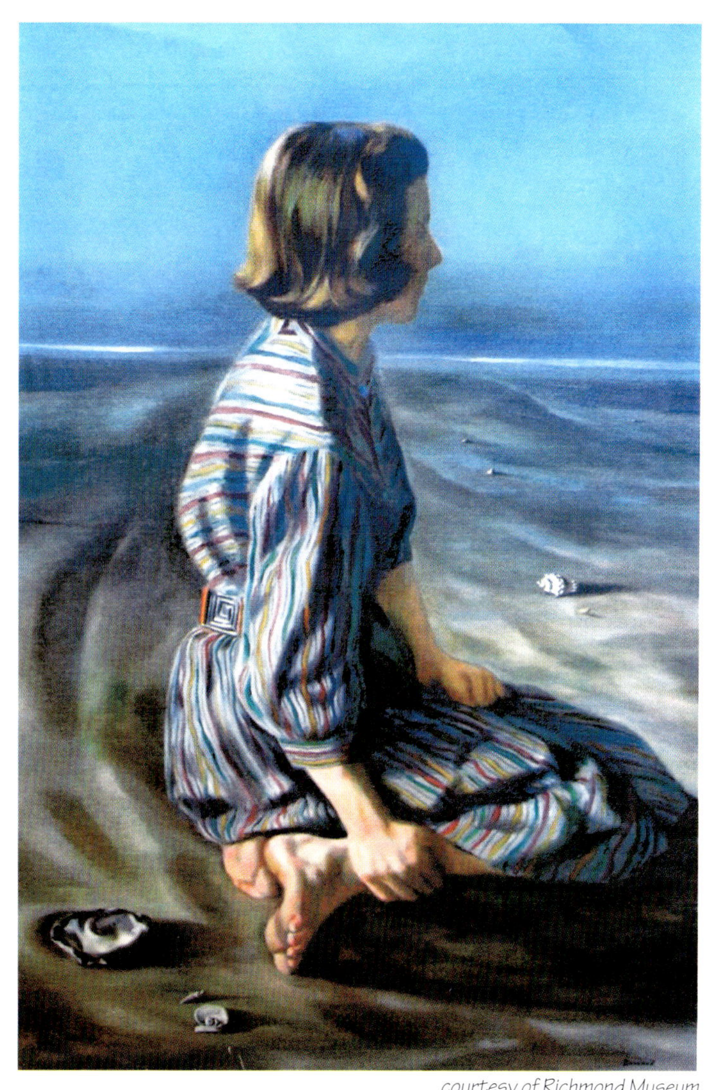

K IN STRIPED DRESS
oil 1954
30x40

Ralph McKelvey, Director of the Art Center in Bradenton, tried a new idea in 1956—a Panel Exhibition in which members of the League were each given panels to fill, making a total of 190 pieces in the show. In his report of the works, Lawrence Dame said of Elden's: "I particularly admire Elden Rowland's oil of fall woods. . . Where some painters merely hang blobs of bright color on sticks to simulate autumn foliage, Rowland, a sensitive and perceptive fellow, makes each detail important and correlated to the other, so that you might take a walk through this forest." Elden gave "Forest" to his mother and I inherited it. Indeed, I often do "go for a walk through the forest," as it hangs above my work space.

Summer of 1956 brought new things for the Rowland Art School, too. At the end of the previous summer, hoping to find a way to avoid the long trip back and forth to The Cape, we decided to search for a place in the mountains of western North Carolina. Early in the Spring I went up from Florida to Hendersonville, taking our artist friend, Margaret Sturgis, with me for company. While I investigated possibilities, Margaret

had a fine time sketching Carl Sandburg's goats, (the famous writer had a home near town). For our school, before going back to Sarasota, I rented an old inn, the Fifth Avenue Villa, at 1312 Fifth Avenue West. Scantily furnished and temporarily closed, it was a rambling structure of 26 rooms and 16 baths, with spacious wooded grounds, large enough to have classes, a gallery, and rent rooms to students as well as to live there ourselves.

In early June we loaded the station wagon and little Nash Rambler, took an art student, Carol Bradley and her friend, J. C., on leave from the military, and went up from Sarasota to turn the inn into an art school. Countless trips up and down the three flights of stairs resulted in shrieking muscles for flatlanders like ourselves but on June 23, 1956, the Rowland Art School, Gallery and Craft Shop opened with a gala reception. We stapled yards of tobacco cloth over the purple and giant white roses of the dining room wallpaper to make a place for a show of Elden's and Carol's paintings and hand-crafted items by mountain artisans.

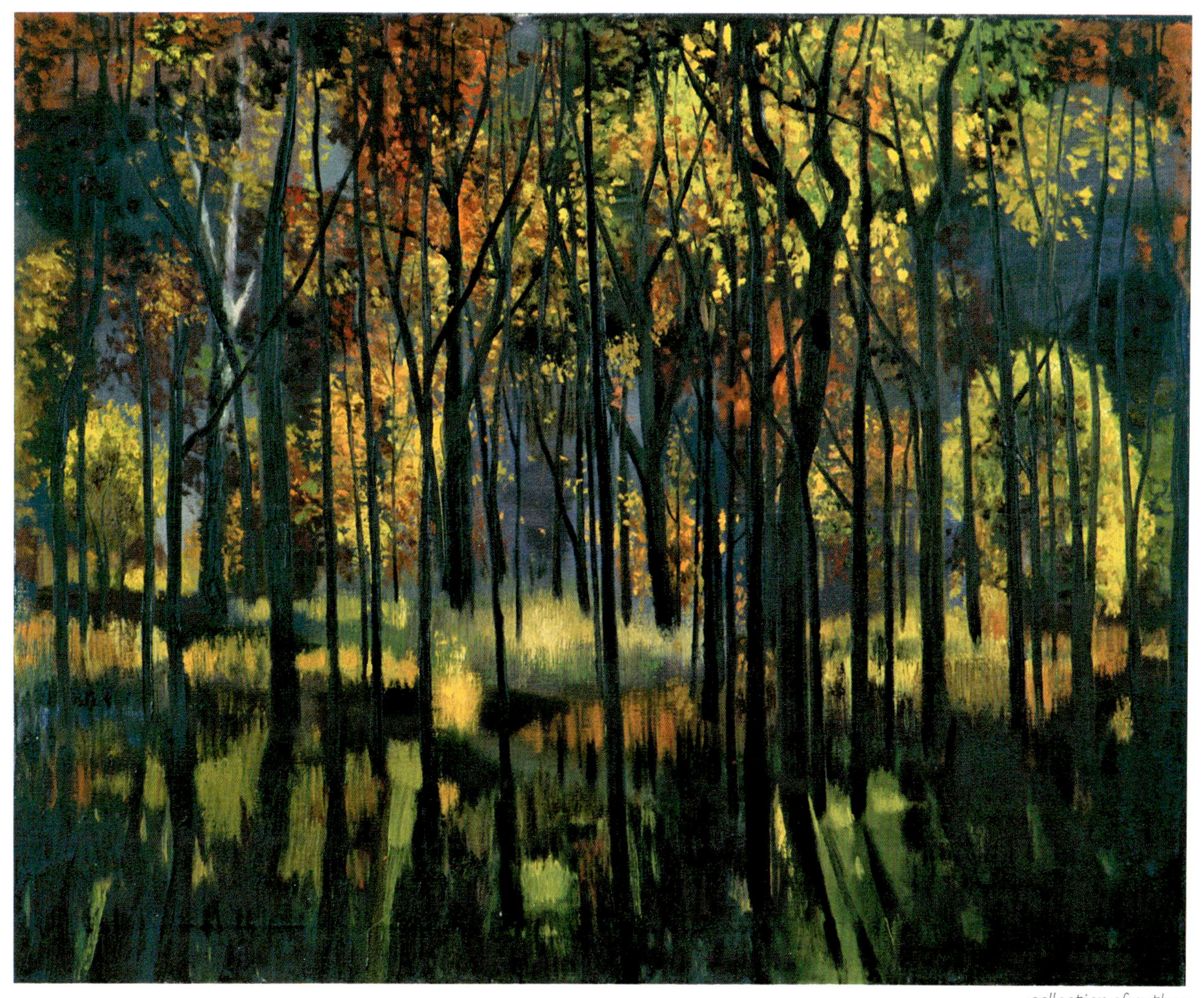

FOREST
oil
30x24

In August of 1956 the Rowland Art School and Gallery in Hendersonville, North Carolina, was proud to present a one-man show of paintings by renowned painter Hilton Leech from Sarasota, Florida. Hilton and his wife, Dorothy, and their four-year old daughter, Jerry, stayed with us at the big old inn over the weekend of the opening. We all enjoyed getting out to walk along a rushing stream to a waterfall, even though we had to shelter under an overhanging rock to avoid a typical sudden mountain shower.

The openings at the Gallery were always a joy to prepare because of the Farmer's Market, for which Hendersonville was famous. The mountain people brought in their harvests of flowers and fruits and vegetables, all very reasonably priced. Every room in the big old inn became colorful and fragrant with fresh bouquets from their gardens and woodlots.

We soon gathered a group of ladies eager to help with the festivities. Christine Hope, a student from Cape Cod, came and spent several weeks. Other students arrived from Cape Cod and Sarasota. Through Eleanor

Hodgins we met Ernestine and Ernest Hamlin Baker, noted *Time* cover artist, who lived in Hendersonville. Mrs. John Forrest, Chairman of the local art group, provided hostesses for the refreshment table.

The Leeches were on their way farther north in the mountains where Hilton was to teach a summer watercolor class. When we first arrived in Sarasota back in 1947-48 we had admired Leech paintings whenever we saw them in shows. Gradually, over the years, through being active in art organizations and being on boards together we came to know each other. Early in 1957 The Bradenton Art League hung a dual Leech/Rowland show in their new galleries. In writing about that show, in the League's yearbook, Lawrence Dame said:

"The Leeches joined in presenting an irresistibly appealing assembly of examples of their recent work. Perhaps the word 'irresistible' should have been reserved for their daughter, Jerry. Young Jerry, confirmed gallery visitor at age four, lends gusto to many a staid art occasion."

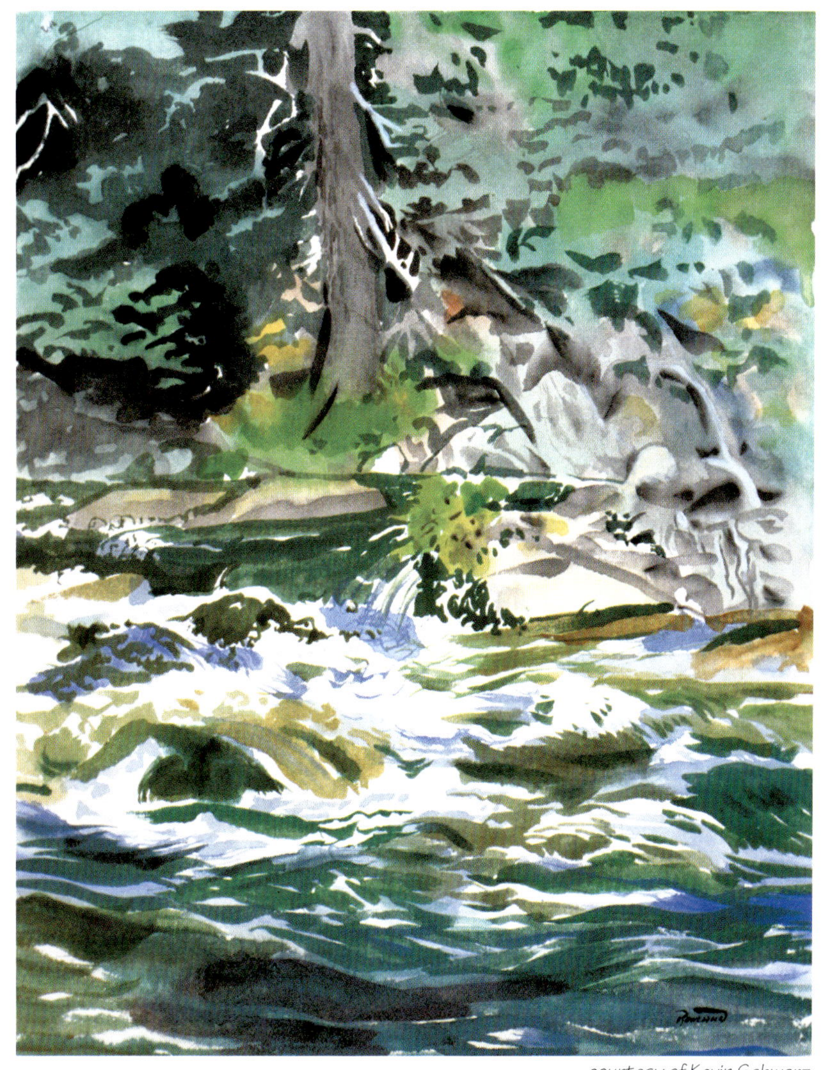

RIVERSIDE WITH TREE
watercolor
25x40

One of the exhibitions at the Rowland Gallery in Hendersonville the summer of 1956 was "*Time* Cover Originals" by Ernest Hamlin Baker. So well-established after 17 years producing these meticulous tempera portraits for *Time*, it was possible for the Bakers to live in the quiet atmosphere of the Carolina mountains while still producing "Journalistic Portraiture" of subjects from President Eisenhower to Marshal Stalin. We were all hopeful that the Bakers' friends, the Carl Sandburgs, could attend the opening but they had other plans. "The *Time* Cover Originals" were later a part of Elden's Traveling Exhibitions.

The rich, velvety blacks of Clare Leighton's nature wood engravings made up another handsome exhibition. A native of England, she became a U.S. citizen in 1946 and fell in love with Wellfleet on Cape Cod. Clare Leighton was renowned as "one of the world's few living masters of the fine art of wood engraving." Unlike woodcuts, wood engravings are cut on the end grain of the wood blocks. The collection was also a part of Rowland Traveling Exhibitions.

Aside from the gallery, the big restaurant-style kitchen was often the favorite place in the house—of the artists—and also, of Smokey, the Cat. Smokey had come to Elden and me one summer through the open doors of the barn studio in Wellfleet. After a vociferous Siamese period of getting acquainted, he gave us his approval and enlivened our lives, whether taking long walks with us or posing like a piece of sculpture high above the kitchen cabinets.

Elden and Carol Bradley and the other students roamed the mountains around town, searching out rushing streams and the highest waterfalls hidden away in Pisgah National Forest. The theme of sparkling water rushing over rocks became one that Elden painted for the rest of his life.

Carol, although still young, was quite an accomplished artist. We had first known her at the Sarasota Art Association. When I worked there and Elden was Exhibition Chairman, there was a policy of giving scholarships to high school students. Carol was one of several.

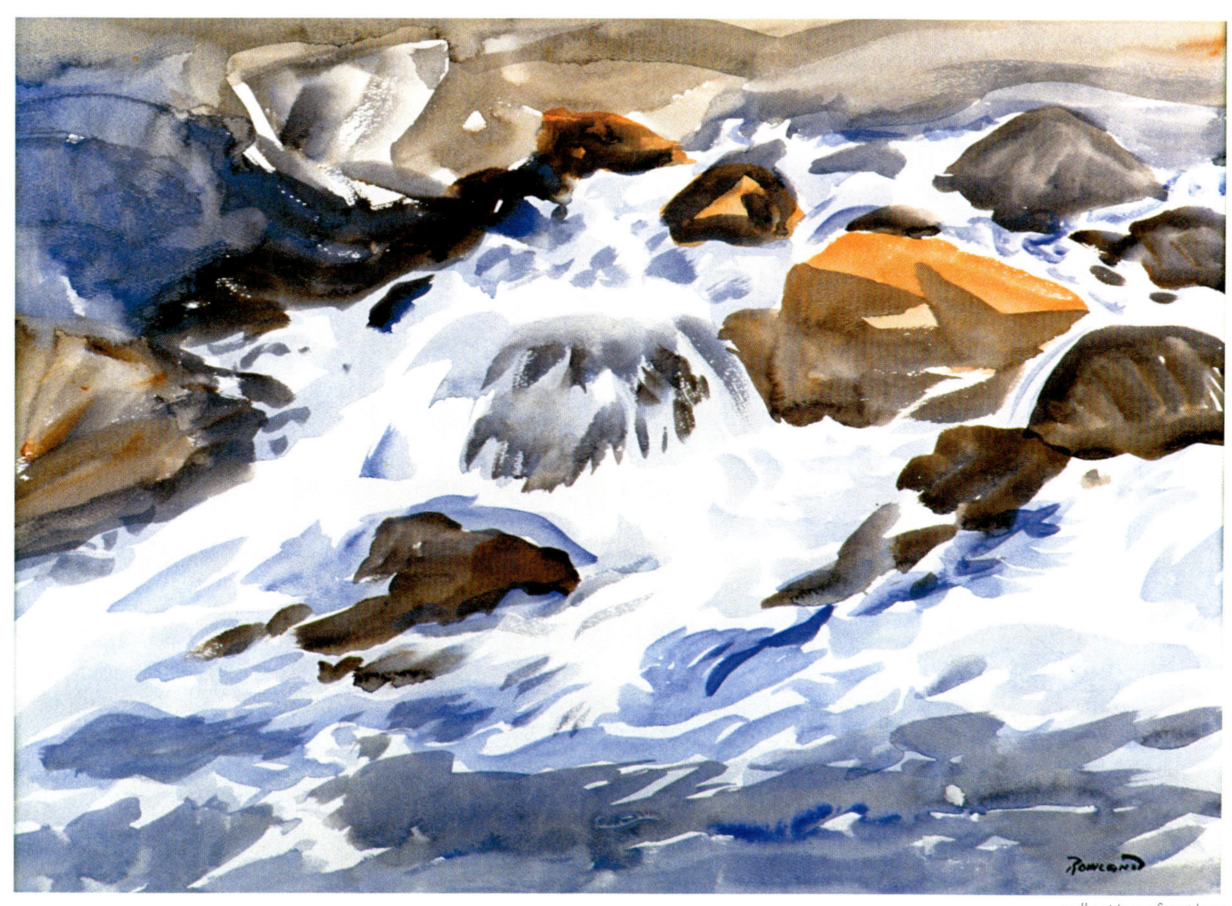

ROCKS & STREAM, BLUE SERIES
watercolor
24x18

When Elden and I returned to Hendersonville in the spring of 1957 the old inn had
been replaced by condominiums. We rented
a summer cottage from a Sarasota attorney
for the early season and then went on to
Cape Cod. Carol Bradley was again with us.

Carol's accomplishments are a story in
themselves. While in high school, she had
won the Florida Federation of Art Scholarship to Hilton Leech's Amagansett Art
School in Sarasota. At the close of her
time with us, we took her to Indianapolis,
Indiana, to start a scholarship at the John
Herron Art Institute. Later she went to
Florida State University at Tallahassee
and continued on to their Center Abroad
program in Florence, Italy. She taught at
Radford College in Virginia and Elden had a
one-man show there. Returning to Florence,
she changed her career to teaching at the
University Linguistic Center, while doing
research, writing and earning a PhD and 2
Masters degrees. In this year of 2006 she
is a freelance online teacher and writer.

Fragmented memories remain of in the
Rowlands' life in the 1950s.

In September of 1954 Hurricane Edna hit
New England while we were still on Cape
Cod. We were living in one of the Apple
Pie Cottages situated on Shirttail Point
thrusting out into Wellfleet Harbor.
With no warning system and no radio, we
didn't realize what was going on and calmly
rode out the shakes and rattles of our
swaying little cottage. Finally, there came a
quiet time so we walked up to get groceries,
although there was no electricity. As we
walked back, the winds returned in all
their fury. We had gone out in the eye of
the storm!

The summer of 1958 I had major surgery
and remember it for the thoughtful
kindnesses showered on me. Eleanor Hodgins
brought me a passion flower blossom every
day at Sarasota Memorial Hospital. Eric
Hodgins saved up his bank statements for
me to reconcile because he knew I loved
doing that. When I found he had $1000
more than he thought he had he gave me a
kiss on the cheek and whipped out his pen to
write me a check. Elden proved his cooking
repertoire could go beyond his specialty of
hot chocolate.

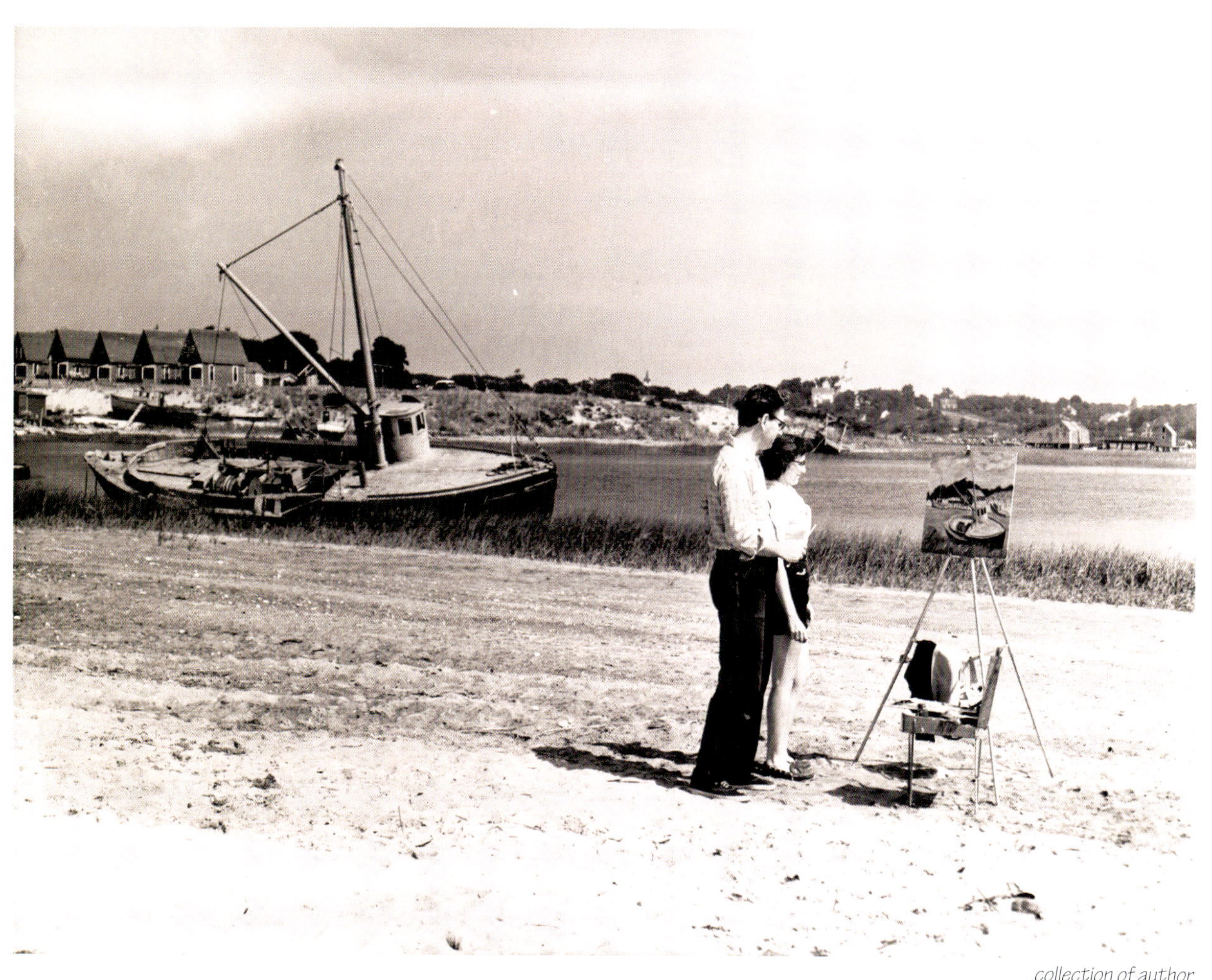

WELLFLEET APPLE PIES
photo b/w
9$\frac{1}{2}$ x 7 $\frac{1}{4}$

"Subjective painting is more important than objective. Can only be done in studio." These two lines in one of Elden's sketchbooks follow two others, "The studio is necessary to control the light on the subject." Adjacent to them is a sketch of a small Cape-Cod-style building with windows down the entire length of one wall.

Perhaps these words were written during a particularly difficult time of helping a student on a typical "in and out" day"—an excuse so often used by students to explain wrongly-placed shadows that it came to denote partly sunny, partly cloudy weather. That, and the additional problems of shifting sands, Wellfleet's high rising and falling tides, and gusting winds, often made painting in the studio seem desirable, even on picturesque Cape Cod. Although Elden had his own north-light workplace on Siesta Key and taught in good studios elsewhere in Florida, in the twelve summers we spent on Cape Cod, we didn't buy property, and he never had a real studio.

Elden almost never wrote anything in his sketchbooks. This unusual instance occurs on a page of tiny drawings of receding mountains (a lesson in perspective) and a sketch of the enigmatic head of a cat.

Cats appear often in the sketchbooks; as do also, drawings of nudes, of his own hands, foliage, and scale drawings of things he was making, like studio easels, or moldings for picture frames, or the Art Nouveau style table he made for our Sarasota dining room. Most pervasive of all, are quick sketches of Katherine: Katherine reading, telephoning, working at a desk, ironing, napping—and posing. Drawings for portraits and the "Girl on the Beach" paintings are scattered throughout the stacks of sketchbooks.

Posing began in earnest for me with the first sound of charcoal on canvas. From then on I needed to hold the pose as nearly as I could as I sat on the collapsible model stand he built. Playing records of classical and boogie-woogie music helped to pass the time. I also learned to place Elden's finished canvases where I could gaze at them, study colors, and follow the intricacies of compositions, and subtleties of color.

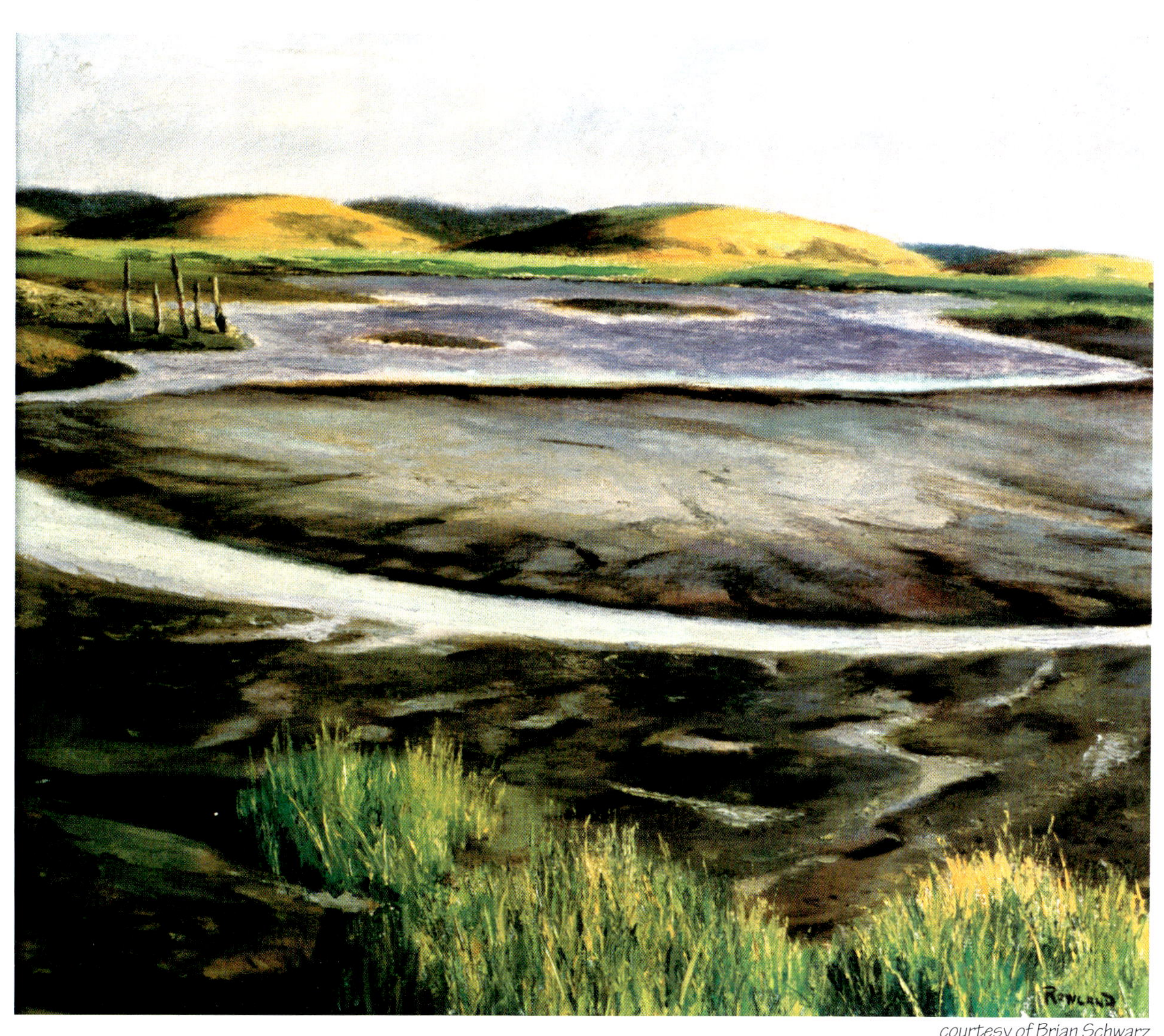

WELLFLEET TIDE FLATS
oil 1952
24x20

93

Many changes came in the Rowlands' life in the 1960s. I had long had an interest in camping and a desire to go Out West. In the summer of 1959 I had considered going to Montana with Margaret Sturgis, who was going out to study with Hilton Leech in the Madison Valley but I decided against it. By making that decision I missed the 7.1 earthquake centered north of Yellowstone Park just before midnight of August 17, 1959. Later I wrote a paper about it, and its earth-changing consequences, for a night class I was taking at Manatee Junior College. The instructor, Mrs. Bryan, gave the paper an "A" and called it "an excellent piece of work, well put-together material," but encircled seven misplaced commas in red.

Larry Lehman, a student at the Leech School in Sarasota, had interested Hilton in going to Montana. Larry had sold a large Colorado property for the Air Force Academy and bought a ranch in The Madison Valley. The Leeches—Hilton and Dorothy, and their daughter Jerry—were living in the parsonage in the small village of Jeffers, across the river from Ennis, central ranching town of the Valley. During the earthquake emergency, they were evacuated to Virginia City above the Valley, at about six thousand feet. Virginia City, center of the mammoth Alder Gulch gold strike in the 1860s and one of the first territorial capitols of the Montana Territory, was an ideal setting for a summer art school. The surrounding mountains were full of beautiful scenery and picturesque old mine settlements for painting excursions. Subsequently, the Leeches bought a two-story log house on a hill overlooking the Madison County Courthouse as their home and headquarters for the art school.

Elden and I decided we would take a camping trip Out West in the summer of 1960. We had a new little Nash Rambler sedan, small for such an adventure, but easy on gas. We bought a car top luggage carrier, an 8 x 8 foot green umbrella tent, sleeping bags, a camp stove and ice chests. I made tote bags out of denim. Later, Elden painted "Pinnacles," which he labeled "Shan Shui," a Chinese term for mountains and trees, but "his own modern abstraction, not like a Chinese painting."

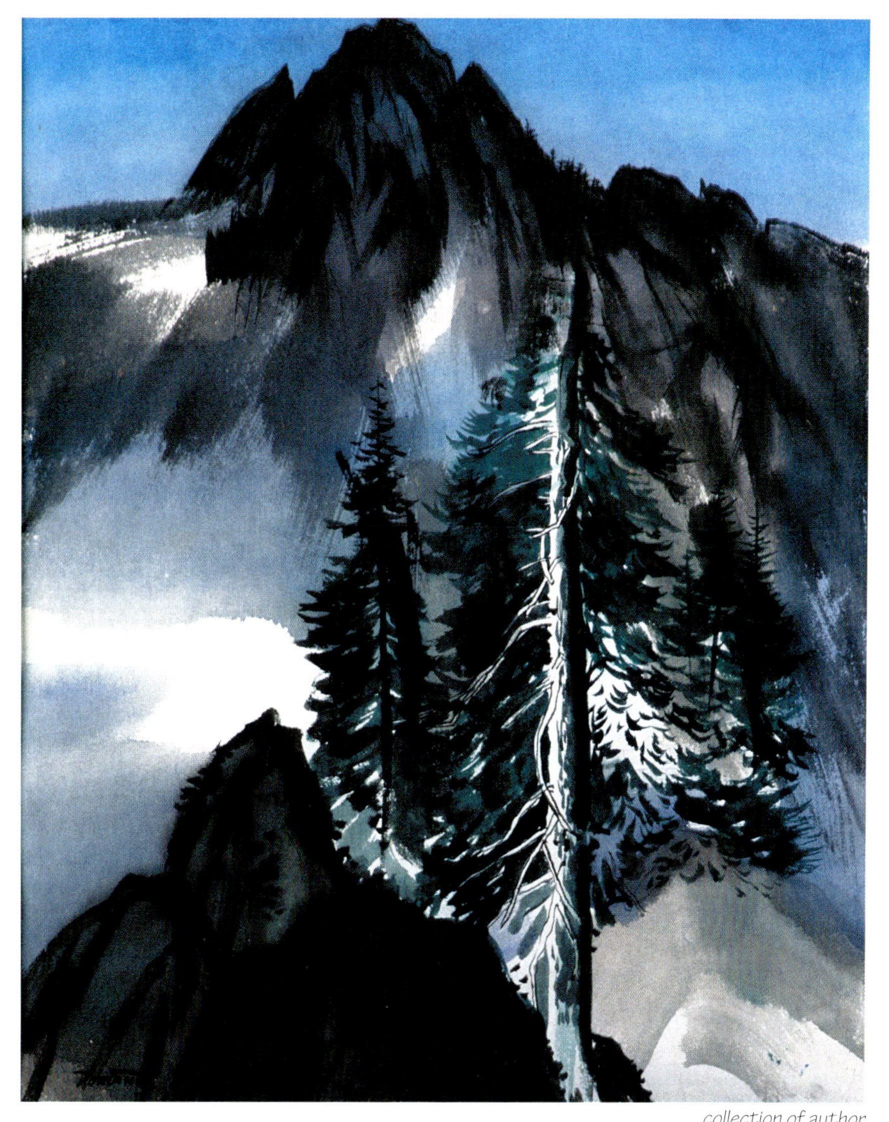

PINNACLES
watercolor
20x24

In the summer of 1960 Elden and I took the first of several camping trips Out West. It lasted six weeks and we spent all but two of the nights with our tent set up in wild, beautiful places. At that time there were few people camping. National parks and forests had designated camping places memorable for their natural beauty, but not for their modern conveniences. We were apt to go out in the morning and find that our neighbor was a moose grazing peacefully nearby or a bear cub climbing a tree, rather than another human being.

We hopscotched our way north and west from Florida enjoying and observing and learning about the myriad of sights and sounds west of the Mississippi River that we had not experienced before. We stopped for a few days to see the Leeches in the Madison Valley of Montana. We visited Hilton's class in the second floor of The Manse, in Jeffers, and found that Margaret Sturgis and Sally Hayden had already arrived. We put up our tent in the fishermen's campground by the River in a grove of cottonwood trees and marveled at the nighthawks plastered vertically against the tall trunks sleeping the days away. Larry Lehman crowded us into his pickup and took us to see his ranch at Wigwam Creek on the west side of The Valley.

After a few days, thinking we might never get West again, we went on toward the Northwest and the Pacific Coast. Elden did not usually paint, nor even draw, as we traveled. However, Oregon, so spectacularly beautiful with its whole coastline reserved for public access, inspired him to do a day-by-day watercolor journal of it in a Japanese accordion-style sketch book. Camping was difficult, entailing Elden's having to carry the tent, etc., down steep hillside through forests of towering evergreen trees, or over the massive trunks of ones that had gone before. The beaches, too, were a tangle of these fallen giants. The huge offshore formations, eroded and sculpted over the ages, gave the whole coast its distinctive appearance and magnetic fascination. Its fascination was enhanced for us by stopping at the high over-looks to see which of us could be first to spot whales migrating from Alaska to Baja California.

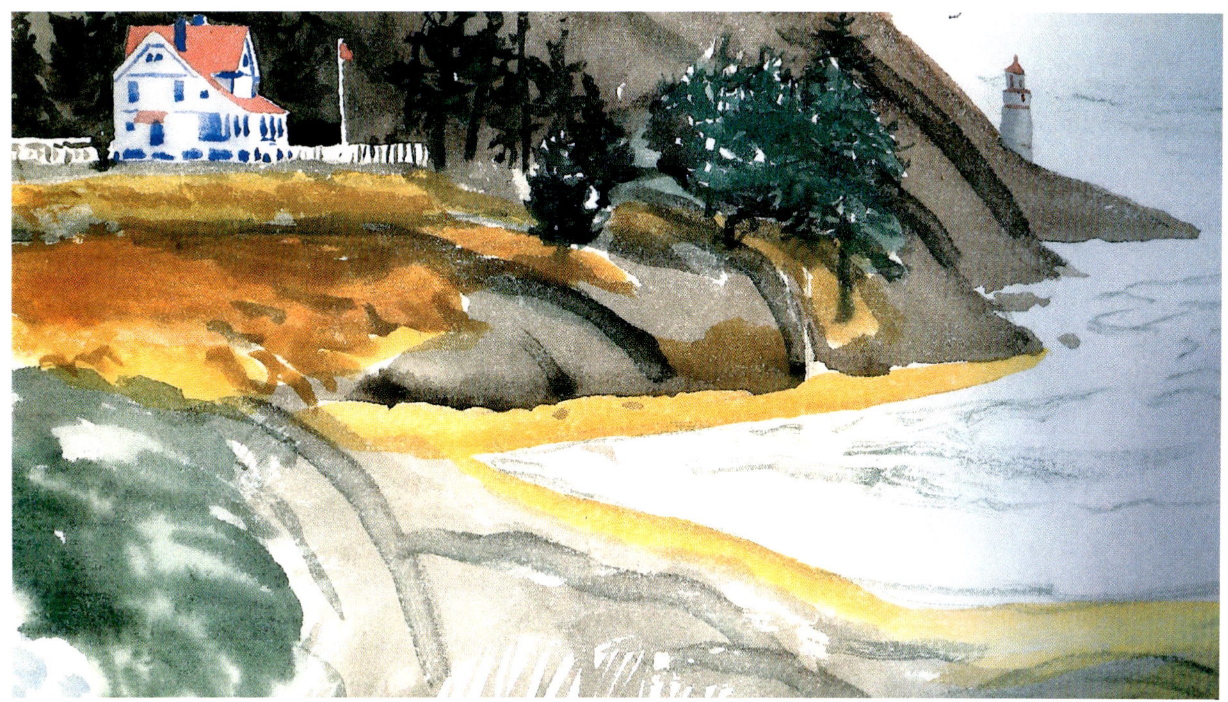

collection of author

OREGON COAST
watercolor sketchbook 1960
8x5

After the lush greenness of the rain forests and giant evergreens of Washington and Oregon, the coast of California seemed quite a contrast to Elden and me on our camping trip in 1960. As we moved south on Rts US 101 and CA 1, the drier climate resulted in high rounded hills covered with golden grass, different from Oregon, also beautiful.

We turned inland to avoid all the cities, except Sacramento. There we visited Elden's relatives whom he had never seen before. During the gold rush of the mid-1800s two of Elden's uncles, the Hageman brothers, left Cincinnati to seek their fortunes Out West and never returned East. Elden's mother kept in touch with her brothers and so we had an address for them. We met one of the uncles and three of Elden's cousins: two men and one woman. The younger of the two men was Louis, named after their ancestor, Captain Louis Hageman of the Union Army in the Civil War. It was a rather uncanny experience because there was a striking resemblance between Louis and Elden. They looked so much alike that the older brother mistook Elden for Louis as he walked toward them.

Continuing through inland California we entered Yosemite National Park from the east over Tioga Pass. The road up to the Pass was in such bad condition that at one point the entire left hand lane has simply disappeared into the valley below, leaving us to wonder whether the right hand lane might follow with us on it. However, we persevered, and reached the top, strewn with huge boulders at over 8,500 feet, before turning back, with gratitude to John Muir, and his Sierra Club, for saving such spectacular country.

Now heading for Florida, we crossed the Mojave Desert, by great good fortune following rare thundershowers. Rainbows appeared before us, touching down in freshly-laundered air and earth where tiny flowers were already beginning to push up and open in colorful display.

Back in Sarasota we went to work as usual, Elden at his painting and exhibiting, I working at J & G Composition, a printing establishment operated by our friends, Jack and Greta Dunnigan, at their house down the street from our home on Siesta.

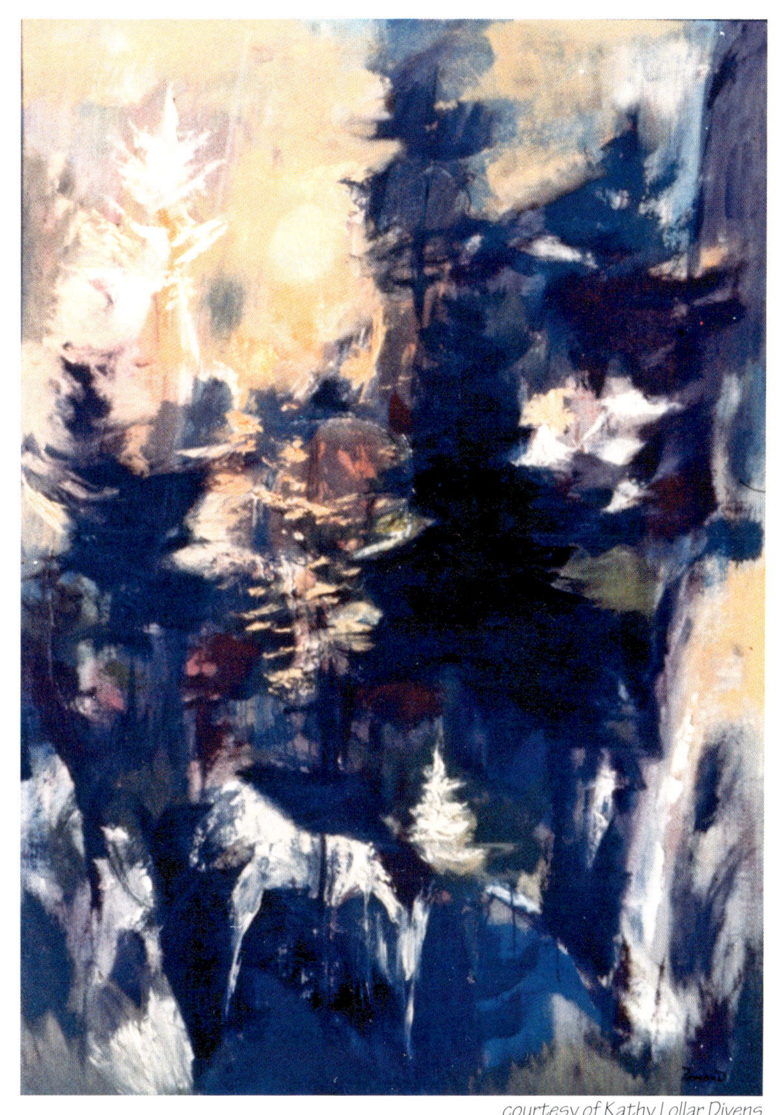

YOSEMITE
oil 1963
36x49

"Yosemite" and "Tioga Pass," two of Elden's paintings from our California trip, had travels that far exceeded our own. They went to Italy in an exhibition "Eight Florida Artists", or, as the invitation said, "Sette Pittori Americani Contemporanei" when it appeared at Galleria XXII Marzo in Venice in October/November 1962. The show was arranged by Rachel Wells Dame, Director of the Palm Beach Branch of Hayes Galleries, NY,

After the show opened in Venice, the United States Information Service, through the American Consulate, asked to circulate it through towns in northern Italy, including Trieste and Verona. The other Florida painters were: Jon Corbino, NA, and Max Bern-Cohen of the West Coast; Artemis Jegart of Jacksonville, and Rachel Wells, Piero Aversa and Henry Faulkner of Palm Beach. Ann Norton, of West Palm Beach showed sculpture. "Tioga Pass" was reproduced in the large soft-cover catalogue.

Both "Yosemite" and "Tioga Pass" were shown extensively before and after their trip to Italy. Prizes at the annual juried Members Show of the Bradenton Art League were something of a "family affair." "Tioga Pass" took top award, with others going to "Stalagmites" by Hilton Leech and "Shaman" by William W. Harris. Bill Harris was a talented student at the Jerry Farnsworth School who lived in Elden's studio a couple of winters.

"Yosemite" and "Tioga Pass" were shown in one-man exhibitions at the Granville Galleries, Coral Gables, Florida, and the Berta Gladstone Galleries in Woodstock, New York. "Tioga Pass" was last seen at a "Lifetime of Work," an exhibition of paintings by Hilton Leech and Elden Rowland at the Art League Of Manatee County in 2001. A commentator called it a "Western Scene with an Asian influence." It was one of several purchased by Michael Lagerman.

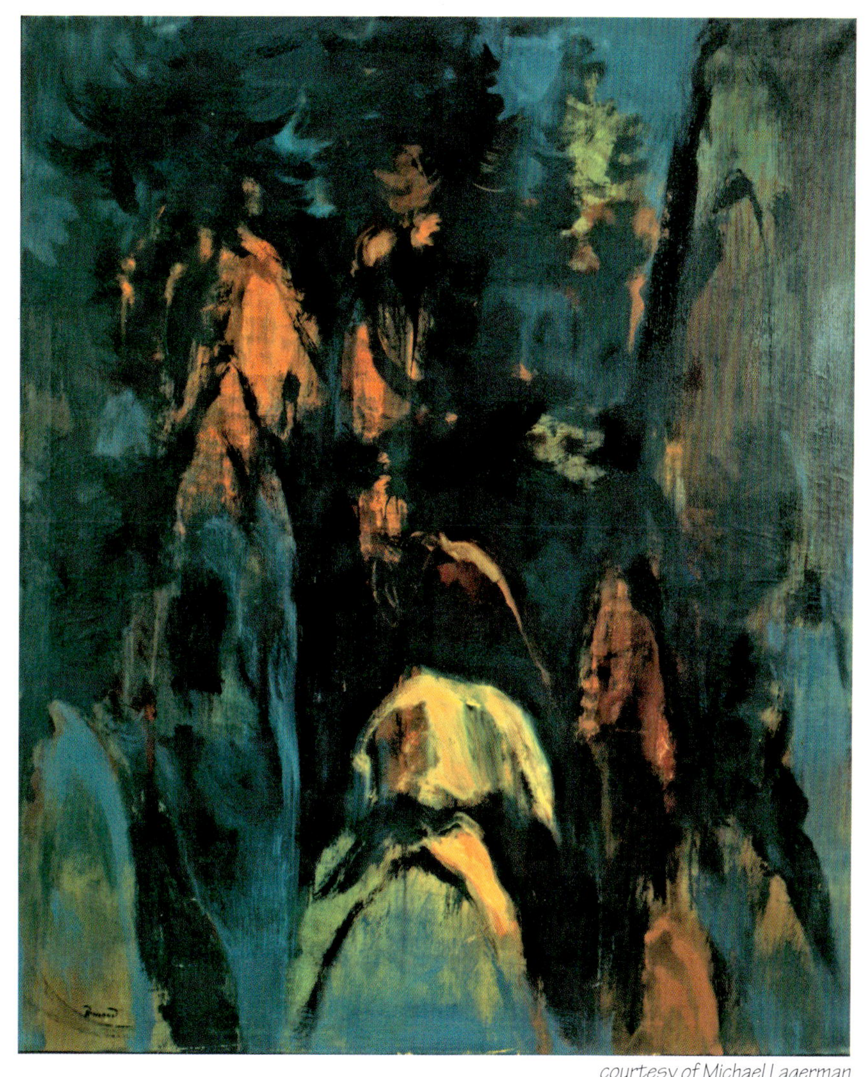

courtesy of Michael Lagerman

TIOGA PASS
oil 1961
42x50

Our 1960 summer camping trip affected Elden and me in many ways. W. C. Burnett, in writing about Elden's work in "Five One Man Shows" at the Sarasota Art Association, noted the change in Elden's painting. (Others in the show were Dorothy Sherman Leech, Loran Wilford, Frank Rampolla, and Sophie Johnstone). Burnett's column in the *Herald-Tribune* on December 27, 1961, says:

"Elden Rowland is a thoughtful painter, and an experimentor. There is some apparent bravura bush work, but is a calculated 'bravura.' He uses many thin washes and modulations which reflect his experimentation in the matter of light striking water, stone and other surfaces. Some of the paintings are shadowy memories, such as 'Oregon Coast,' in which he has recalled the rocks and the water. The paintings could be viewed by many as abstractions, and maybe some would claim that they are non-objective. They aren't, however. As they are minute observations of nature, they may well be termed representational, too. I think that he is now more successful than in the past, because he is not quite as preoccupied with problems of design. The best paintings have a more natural and more vital structure."

That fall of 1960, Elden had one-man shows at Gainesville, Tampa and St. Petersburg. "Monterey Cypress," one of the California series, got an honorable mention in the Florida Artists Group 15th Annual Exhibition. He won an award in the prestigious Contemporary American Paintings exhibition at the Society of the Four Arts in Palm Beach. It was a bonus that we enjoyed driving around Florida delivering paintings—Elden's entries and those of other Sarasota artists.

This was the beginning of a list of 14 awards Elden's work won during the 1960s. All of the paintings were influenced by trips West. We went out again the summer of 1961, spent more time with the Leech art classes, rented Mrs. Gohn's house in Virginia City down the hill from the Leeches'. It had been a miner's home, had a bathroom, but no hot water, was sparsely furnished with cots and an old school desk for my typewriter—camping under a roof, with lilacs in bloom by a ruined log cabin next door.

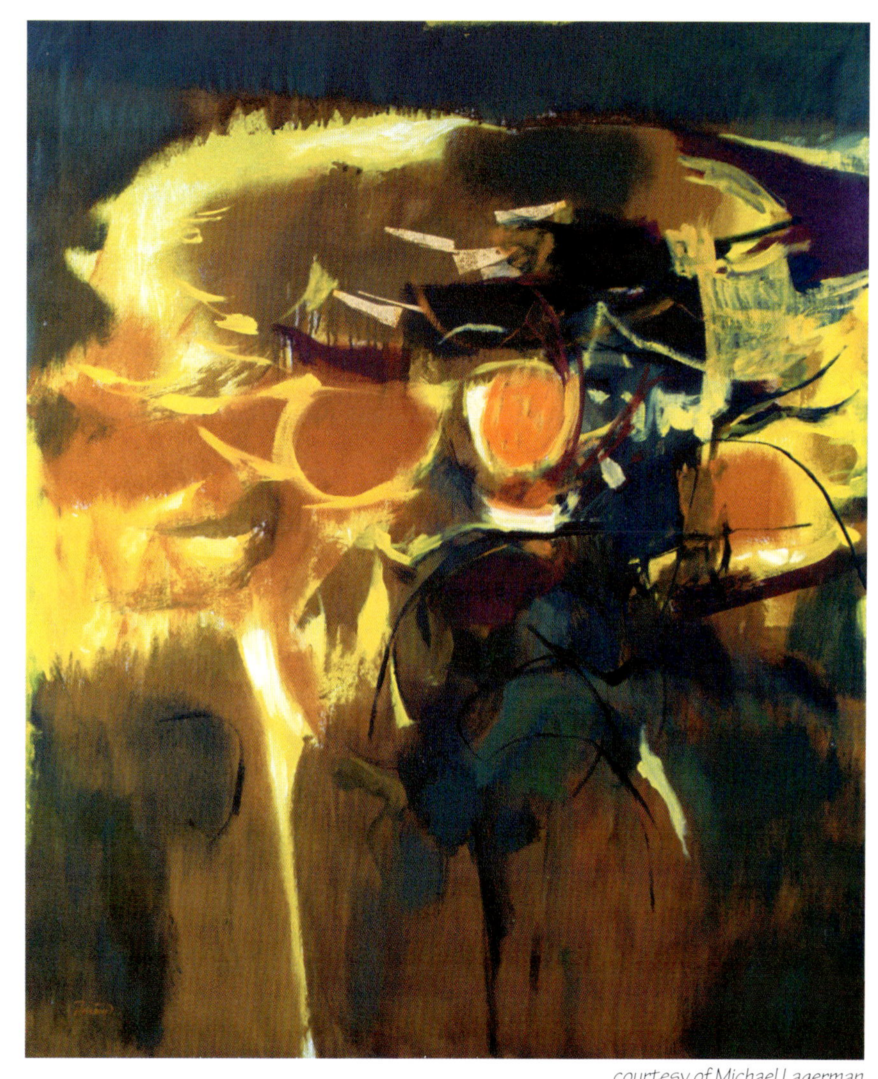

courtesy of Michael Lagerman

MONTEREY CYPRESS
oil
44x52

One summer when we were in Virginia City Hilton Leech asked Elden if he would like to teach at his winter Art School in Sarasota. Elden was happy to accept.

After the Leeches returned to Sarasota at the end of their jobs in a World War II war plant in the north, Hilton started the Amagansett School at 1666 Hillview Avenue. Around 1960 they bought property on the south edge of town at 4344 Riverwood Avenue to build a new school and home. The name was changed to The Hilton Leech Art School. The new studio was an innovative round two-story masonry and glass building designed by architect Jack West,

A few years earlier Hilton's broad interest in the natural world led him to have Roger Early, a popular science lecturer from Brandon, Florida, teach at the Leech School. Hilton's instruction focused on a series of Monday morning demonstrations in watercolor and landscape classes. Roger's "Science Demonstrated" lectures were planned to help attendees understand all the complexities of the just-emerging Space Age. Elden taught a studio workshop

in traditional oil techniques, leading toward creative expression. I occasionally did secretarial work for Hilton.

A group of enthusiasts who gathered around Hilton and Roger bought a 16 mm projector and rented movies for a Monday evening series of art and science films at the Studio. This group expanded its programs and grew in numbers to a total of 73 persons when it was chartered on March 7, 1963, as The Friends of the Arts and Sciences, a non-profit, educational organization. Elden and I were charter members. For the next four decades The Friends shared the Leech Studio with the Hilton Leech Art School.

The next season after the Friends of the Arts and Sciences was chartered I became full-time secretary for the expanding programs of the two groups at the Leech Studio. Sally Hayden joined the teaching staff. Gordon and Emily Holmes, he an engineer and she an artist, became active and important parts of both organizations as well as valued friends to the Leeches and Rowlands.

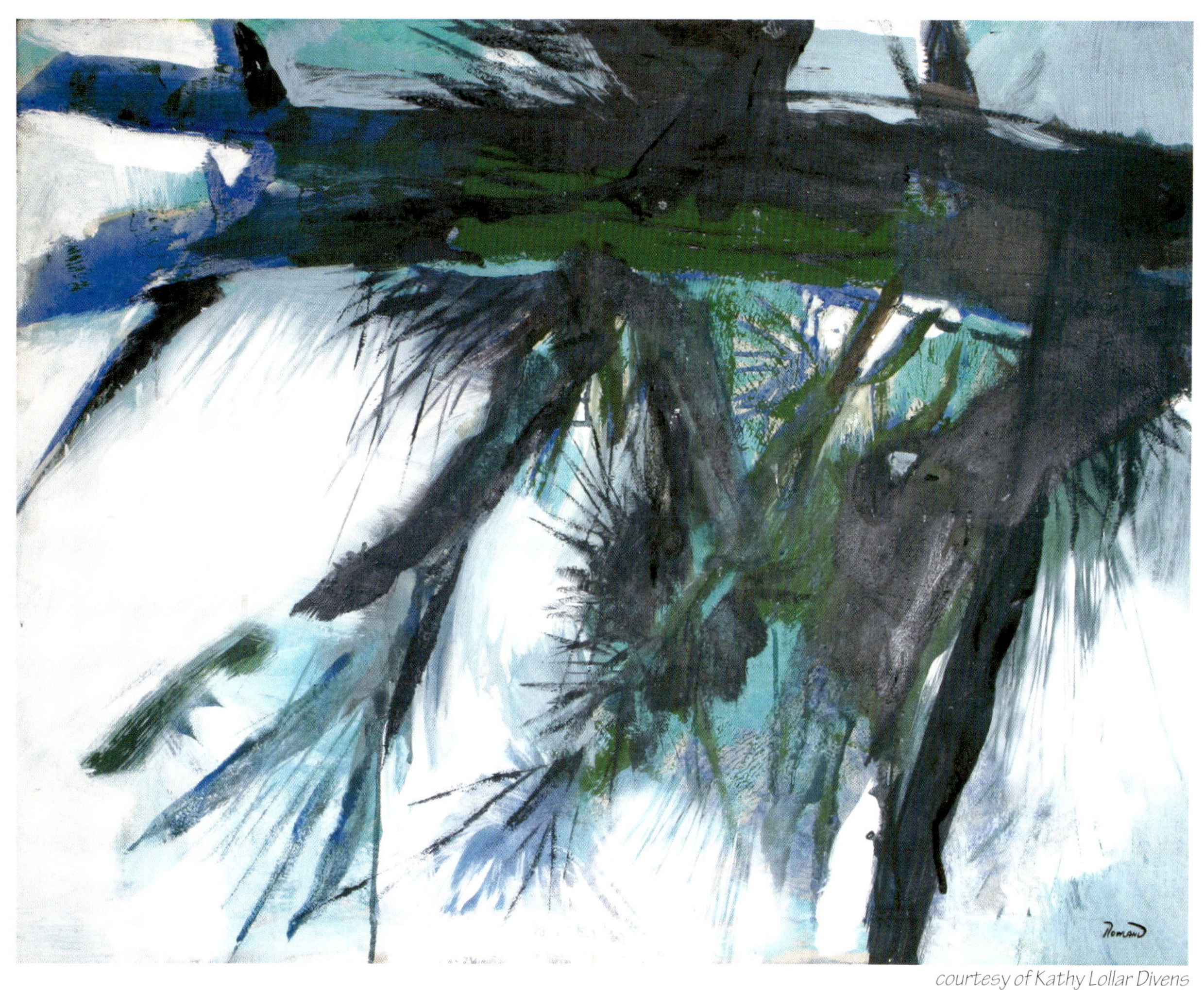

courtesy of Kathy Lollar Divens

BIG PINE
oil 1965
36x28

The Beaux Art $350 purchase award was given to Elden's entry in the 10th Annual Exhibition of the Joe and Emily Lowe Art Gallery, May 1963. The painting went into the permanent collection of the Gallery at the University of Miami, Coral Gables, Florida. The title of the painting is "Storm," although Elden's correspondence with the Director, C. Clay Aldridge, whom he knew from his Traveling Exhibition, calls it "Landscape with Tree."

Allied Publications of Fort Lauderdale chose this painting to be included in Book III of *Prize Winning Paintings* and requested 4x5 color transparency which Lowe Gallery provided. The printing of a reproduction of a painting is a tricky business. The transmittal of light and color through the artist's mind to his brush and canvas, through the photographer's mind and lens to the film, and through the printer's mind to inks and paper, is fraught with peril. In this case, Elden was resigned to the fact that it was "out of his hands," but did comment "they have developed the blue and pretty well lost the warm colors and the blacks. The blacks in this painting are really solid black, not dark blues; also the painting has some areas of green which do not show up well at all." In the book, it is upside down!

Statement of juror E. E. Ulman says: "I like the immediate dramatic tension in this mysterious painting—the richness and harmony of the color was successfully evocative." Elden's artist's statement says, in part:

"This painting is one that flowed easily from my sub-conscious mind. I began by thinking of the blank canvas as an actual part of my own mind, rather than as something external, and activated it by applying a horizontal band of thin color across the top, without visualizing any subject. From this, it grew into a landscape, no doubt remembered from many landscapes. The idea of calligraphy entered into it in the painting of the tree, which, like perspective, is a part of my technical equipment. Nevertheless, this painting remains a completely spontaneous expression of my own inner feeling for both landscape and painting. . . or, one might say—for nature and art."

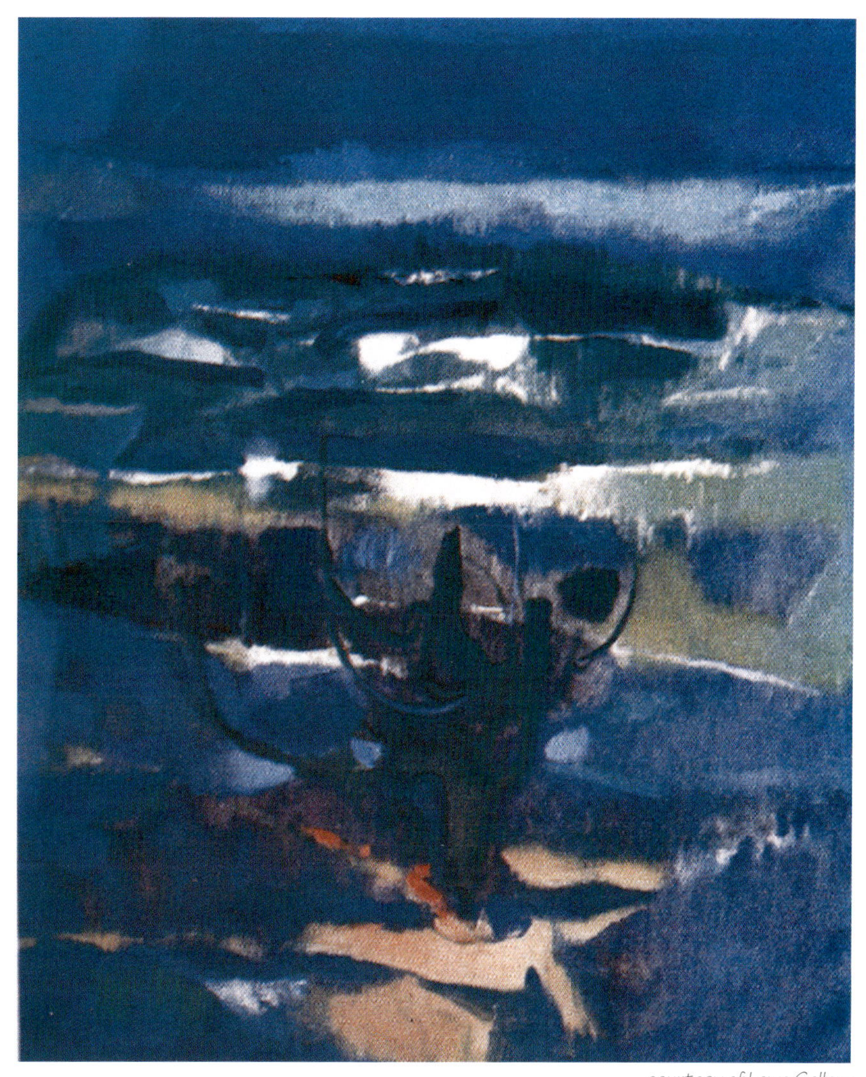

STORM
oil 1963

"Diffuse Abstractionist" was a term used to describe Elden by Doris Reno, Music and Art Editor for the *Miami Herald,* in commenting on his show at Granville Galleries, Coral Gables, in May of 1961. In an article illustrated by a photograph of "Mystery of Time," she said: . . . a style which "floats' colors into one another in soft, unoutlined shapes. . . He is intending to suggest to the mind self-propelled images of 'spring rain,' 'rain-cloud,' and 'reflections'. . . . by diffused color-clouds arranged as poetically as possible. There are no definite lines, no tautness, in the canvases; everything melts, flows away. . . this painting has the firmest, contoured outlined shapes."

Elden, himself, called the painting "abstract-expressionist." It was later exhibited under the title "Arctic Dawn" and was purchased by Eleanor Book of Siesta Key.

A roster of Elden's work reveals a number of ways he explored the possibilities of expression. He did a series of collages, saturating small pieces of Japanese paper in pure color before clipping them to long clotheslines in the studio to dry. He made prints from such things as seagrape leaves and bamboo shoots, and did exquisite Oriental calligraphy to be collaged in. He had a technique of crumpling pieces of newsprint on top of an almost-finished painting and setting it on fire, leaving rich black ashes—a sure attention-getter at a demonstration.

When Elden was teaching at The Colony on Longboat Key, another artist was working with stained glass. This inspired Elden to do a large stained-glass mosaic, which he gave to Hilton and Dorothy Leech as a house-warming present for their new home on Pine Terrace.

He took classes with Frank Colson in pottery and lost-wax sculpture and made 8 small pots and wax models of a nude and a horse. The wax models were never cast in bronze, as was intended. One time while I was away planning a Western group tour, Elden carved a bison for me out of steatite (soapstone), a dark green piece brought back from an earlier trip, soft and easy to carve, but with a tendency to fracture.

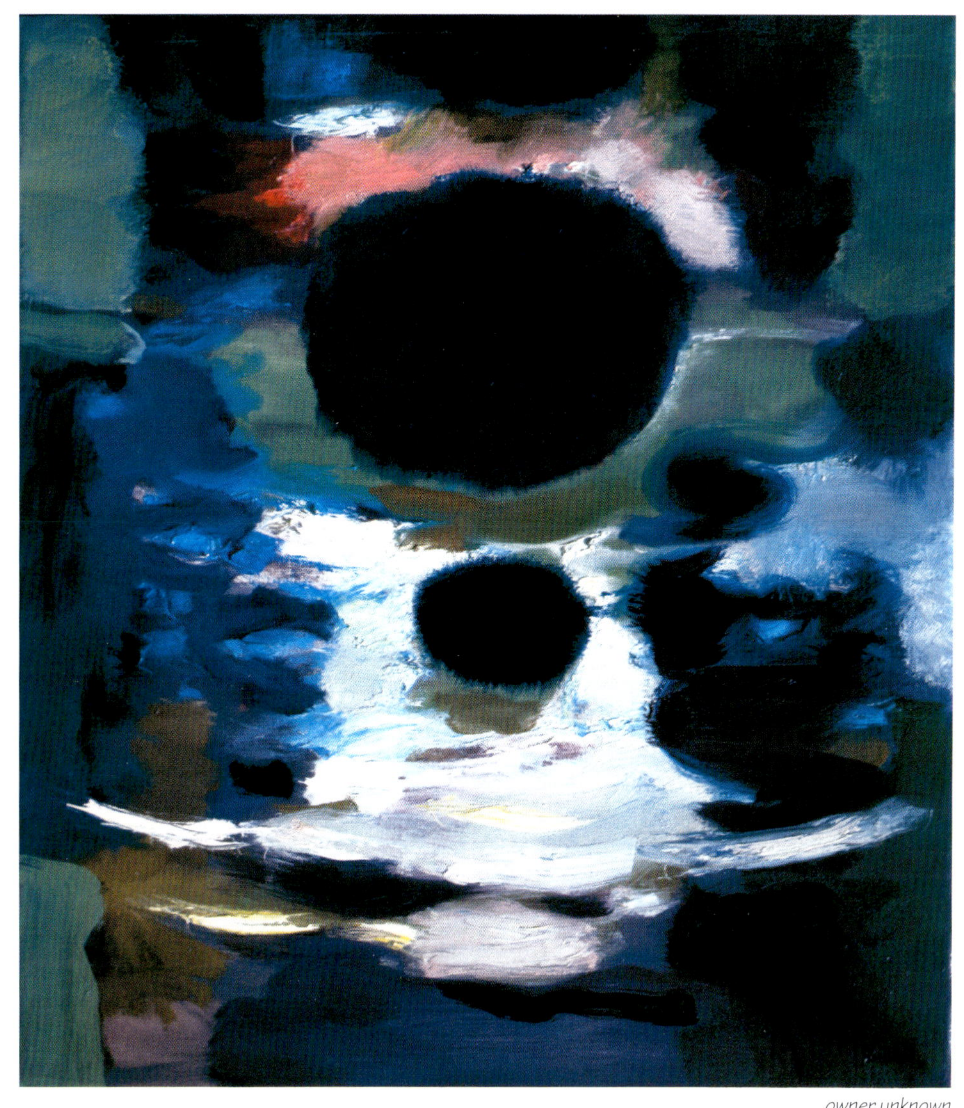

owner unknown

MYSTERY OF TIME
oil 1961

Elden and I varied our routes to and from Montana summers in the early 1960s so we could visit all the national parks. We went to several pre-historic sites, including Mesa Verde in southwest Colorado. His painting "Kivas" was inspired by the Anasazi ruins.

The Sarasota Art Association sponsored a South Coast Art Show, open to artists from nine southeast states, some invited, some subject to jury. The show was hung in the Ringling Museum and opened with a gala reception on January 7, 1961. The spiked punch was prepared ahead of time in a five-gallon water jar, and taken to the Ringling family crypt that served as the "kitchen." Unfortunately the giant jar was dropped, spilling punch all over the crypt floor, much to the consternation of the refreshments committee!

Nevertheless, the show went on. "Kivas," a juried entry, received one of ten equal $50 honor awards. Ryder System, Inc., of Miami established a $3,000 purchase fund and sponsored a traveling exhibition through William Moise, an Art Association board member and a Ryder executive.

Elden was one of three Sarasota painters whose work was purchased, the others being Beth Arthur and Syd Solomon. The three were among 30 pieces chosen by Kenneth Donahue, Director of the Ringling Museum to travel to six museums through the southeast. Other Sarasotans were Robert Larsen, Hilton Leech, and Richard Oxley. The catalog was designed by Elden as part of his traveling exhibitions, using a Rorschach design, which he was exploring as a painting motif during that time. Elihu Edelson's review in *The News* said: "'Kivas' is an offbeat performance by this painter of many styles. The blanched images, strange hues, and narrow range of values may relate to Rowland's interest in photography."

One Sunday afternoon that summer in Montana, I went with Hilton Leech and Elden to pan for gold outside Virginia City. I soon grew tired of that heavy sloshing back and forth of gravel in freezing water to look for tiny specks of "color," and wandered off exploring. I happened upon a large area strewn with old purple bottles shining out among the sagebrush. I had found the historic town dump!

collection of author

SOUTH COAST ART SHOW
catalog 1961
5$^{1}/_{2}$ x 8$^{1}/_{2}$

One fall, Hilton and Dorothy Leech went to Hamilton, Ontario, so Hilton could do enamel-on-steel murals for Dofasco, a large iron works owned by Dorothy's family, the Shermans. Elden and I took their daughter back to Sarasota with us. Jerry and her cat were both good camper-travelers.

The summer after I found the historic City Dump, the Rowlands had a Bottle Shop. We rented the old bank building in the center of Virginia City. A little red brick building, complete with the original bank vault, it was, in itself, of interest to the streams of visitors who browsed up and down the main street, hardly able to tell which buildings were restorations of the gold boom days, and which were the few currently-operating businesses.

That summer we took Donna Smith with us Out West. A talented young Sarasota woman who was a student at the Hilton Leech School, Donna did attractive woodcuts that were also displayed in the Bottle Shop, along with small carvings that Elden did of gleaming white gypsum we found in roadcuts as we traveled.

Donna had an interest in riding horses, making the Western atmosphere a natural for her. She soon met a handsome young man, John Impero, who was visiting relatives in the nearby ghost town of Nevada City. Donna did not go back to Florida with us, but went on to the Northwest where she and John were married.

Elden and I went back to Sarasota in late August so he could go North to teach workshops in New York State and Connecticut, which he continued to do, spring and fall, for the next ten years.

Elden had always liked to draw, especially the human figure. He attended the classic "life drawing classes" wherever they were available. He also continued to experiment to find new techniques and new combinations of the old and the new. In "Oval" he superimposed a drawing of a nude from one of his many sketchbooks onto a textured background of sand—sand which he obtained by bringing back buckets full from the beach near our place on Siesta Key and carefully sifting it and washing it and drying it.

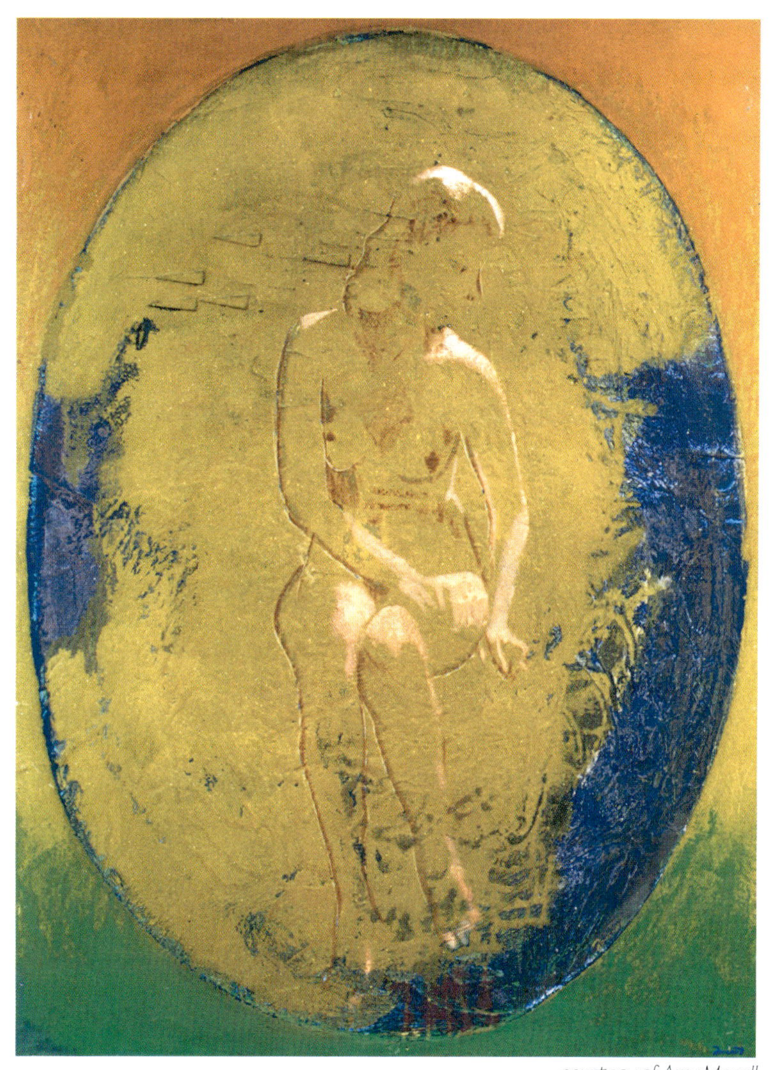

OVAL
oil on sand
38x50

As the programs of the Friends of the Arts and Sciences and Leech Art School expanded in the middle 1960s, I became completely involved in planning and carrying out arrangements for events. FAS grew rapidly in membership and scope of interesting activities. It soon had programs three nights a week: a drawing clinic, a movies night, and art and sciences programs, alternating weekly. After starting modestly with field trips in Florida, they decided to have "foreign" tours in the United States and abroad.

In April of 1966 the first "foreign tour" went to the Yucatan Peninsula of Mexico to visit the ruins at Chichen Itza and Uxmal and learn about the civilization of the Maya. Travel arrangements were made by Pat Matthews of Travel, Incorporated. Pat, and her husband Dr. Lamar (Nappy) Matthews, close friends of Hilton and Dorothy Leech, often went with the groups. However, they were unable to go on this first one, and I was designated the Tour Leader. I was pleased to accept the task but with fear and trepidation, because I had never been out of the United States before, had

never been on an airplane, and did not speak Spanish. However, all went well, thanks to Hilton's help and guidance.

With a variety of titles, I continued at FAS and the Hilton Leech Studio for almost a quarter of a century. It became a way of life, a challenging opportunity for growth for me, particularly in the world of travel. Gaining experience through the one-day field trips, I learned to plan and escort group tours throughout the United States and Canada. Often I went on exploratory journeys, mapping out the smallest details. Occasionally Elden would go with me on the exploratory trips, especially if I was doing it during the Christmas break of The Studio.

Elden continued to enjoy experimenting in his artwork. He did a series incorporating rubbings into the painting. The rubbings were usually of leaves and other plant material. In "Satyr" he went a step further and did a rubbing from a plaster head kept in the Leech Studio for drawing practice. In that same period, he was also using gold —gold paper backgrounds, gold leaf, and washes of gold paint.

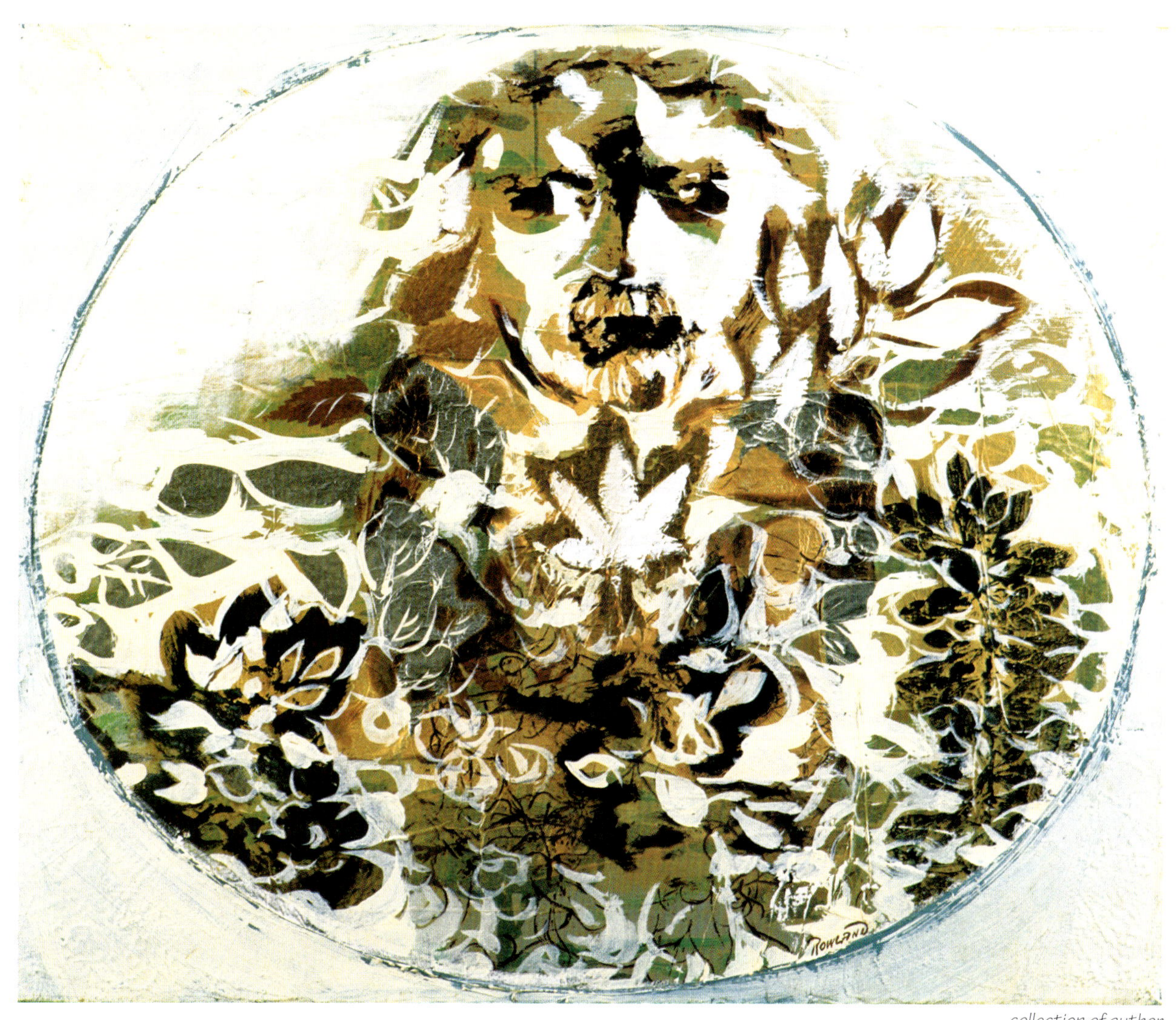

collection of author

SATYR
collage 1969
24x20

Elden was eager to secure a gallery in Sarasota, one that would represent his work and aggressively promote its sale. This was difficult because galleries preferred the work of artists who consistently painted in one recognizable style. Elden's passion for experimentation and exploring different media made them feel that his work was not "collectible." Although he had a one-man show at Murray Lebwohl's St. Armand's Gallery and occasionally had pieces hung in the Oehlschlaeger Gallery, also on St. Armands Key, he began to look further afield. In Florida, he showed at The Messina Gallery in Ft. Lauderale, the Granville Gallery, in Coral Gables, and Garrisons' Gallery in Ft. Myers.

Berta Gladstone, a Sarasota resident, opened a gallery in Woodstock, New York, and Elden took work there many years. He had one-man shows in museums at Greenville, South Carolina, and Columbus, Georgia. He began to spend summers teaching workshops and painting in The East. Although he enjoyed being with the Leech Montana art group, he did not feel inspired to paint there, feeling more personally drawn to the sea than the mountains.

I continued to drive to Montana. One summer I took Elsinore Budd and her little dog Susie, our dear friends from Cape Cod days. Another year, I took Eleanor Fair and Bonnie Bausor. Eleanor, a retired librarian from New York City, was a delight—in person, and in her instinctively beautiful watercolors. Bonnie, an Antioch, Ohio, off-campus student, was a bright spirit who linked the generations together and kept us all in stitches.

Winters in Florida were times of interesting activity. The Friends of the Arts and Sciences did a scientific exploration of an Indian mound in Englewood. There was a Creative Modern Ikebana show with plant arrangements by Carol Baumgartner and her students, interpreting paintings by Hilton and Elden. Carol and Elden did a huge arrangement for the courtyard. A Shapes-in-Gold Show, included "Bird Screen," one of several screens Elden made combining his enjoyment of working with wood and his love of exploring media and methods.

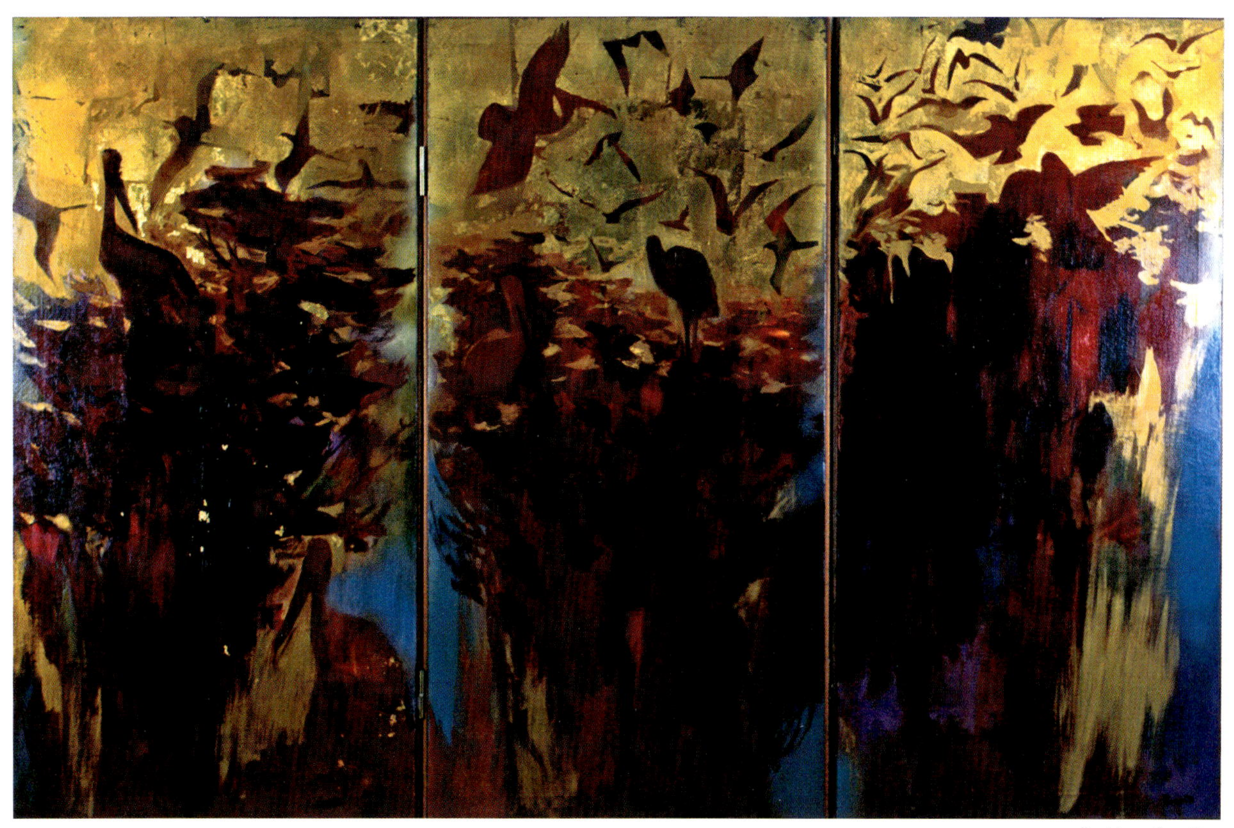

collection of author

BIRD ROOKERY SCREEN
oil 1966
78x50

Taking photographs was an important part of my life in the 1960s. For $25 I found a used Zeiss Ikon Contina 35 mm camera. It had minimal manual adjustments of lens opening and focal distance but it took beautiful pictures in spite of my inexperience in photography.

Summers in Montana were full of photo opportunities—the magnificent mountains surrounding wide valleys, the fascinating ghost towns and tailings from old gold dredges, the endless blue sky and dramatic clouds, rainbows coming down in Alder Gulch —all were irresistible! At least one day a week the Leech art group went to a choice spot on an all-day picnic. Other days were spent rock hounding or simply exploring, being sure to keep wheels on one side of the station wagon on top of the rocks, to avoid dragging the oil pan. Some evenings, after the spectacular light effects drained from the sky at the Leeches' house on the top of the hill in Virginia City, we gathered and looked at my slides—my little niche in a world of painters!

Elden and I spent short periods in Colorado. Together, we attended a Wildlife Federation Summit at Estes Park. Elden's painting "Shining Mountain" came from that experience. I took a course at the University in Boulder, first of several summer short courses in other places. In the days before Elderhostel, that gave me a chance to learn about different areas and meet "real" college students.

Back in Sarasota, the Friends of the Arts and Sciences groups took several Spring trips to Mexico and Guatemala, following the interest in the culture of the Maya. Those of us who took slides pooled them for group showings at the Leech Studio. In the spring of 1969 the Friends' tour was to Ecuador and the Galapagos Islands. I was scheduled to go only on the Ecuador portion. That in itself was a memorable experience: the capitol city of Quito with colorful Indian markets, an electric train trip over extremely high mountains, long waits for little red engines to steam by on the way down to the west coast port of Guayaquil.

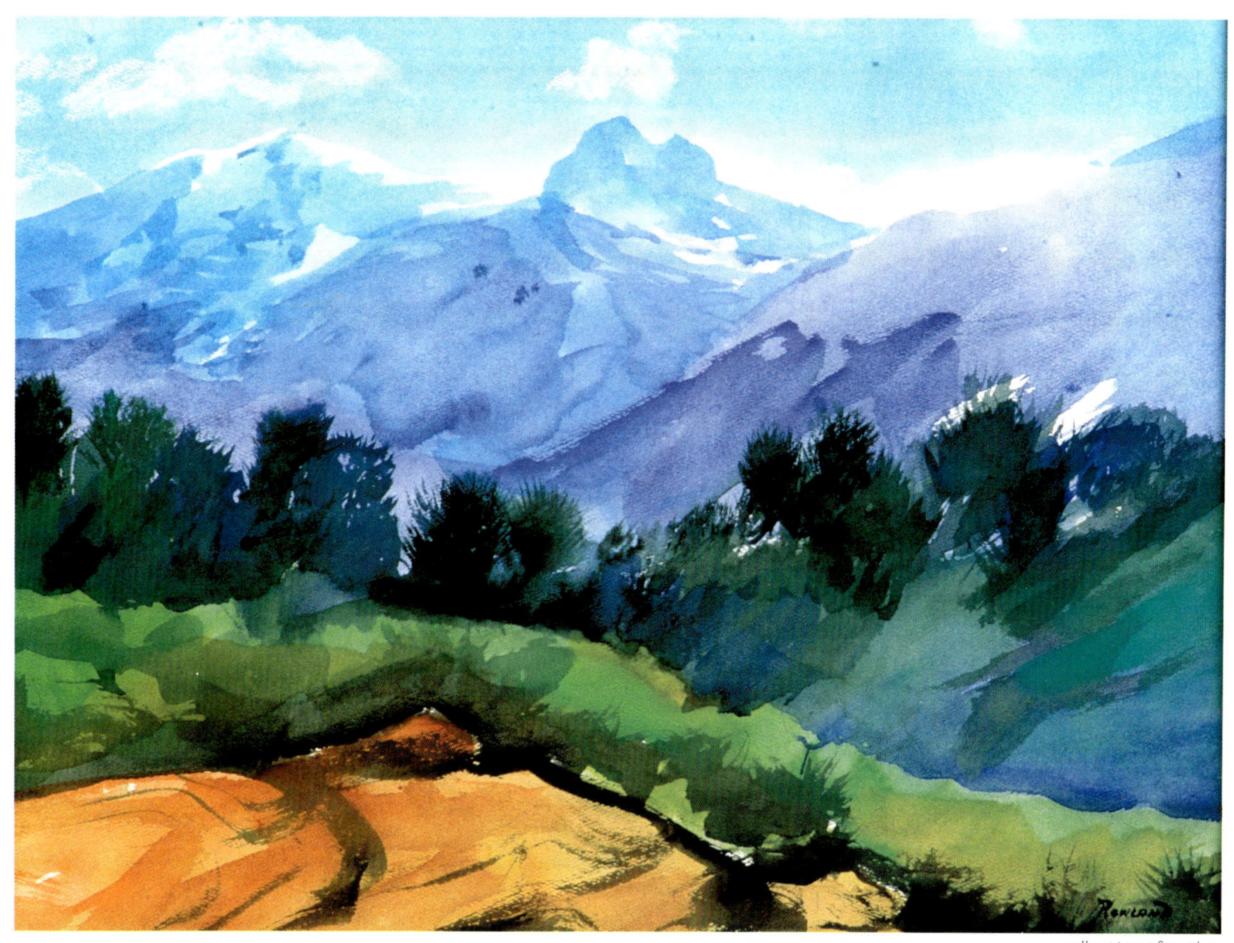

collection of author

SHINING MOUNTAIN
watercolor
18x24

I went to the Galapagos Islands in the Spring of 1969 although I had not expected to. The Leeches and Pat Matthews returned to Florida by way of New Orleans so Hilton could have check-ups at a clinic. I escorted the rest of the group on the trip home.

Tourism to the Galapagos Islands was just beginning to develop in 1969. We were flown from Guayaquil on the private plane of the leader of Ecuador, and taken by small boats to the different islands. Our main accommodation was on Santa Cruz, near the Darwin Research Station. One of our tour guides was Tui DeRoy, young daughter of a French family of settlers. Tui later became well-known for her photography of the Galapagos.

Our group was to go by horseback to a farm high in the hills of the island. I tried riding one of the little island horses with a saddle that was really just a leather pad, but the horse's stumbling gait seemed designed to throw me forward over his head, so I elected to walk, in spite of the sharp lava. As the days went on, Hilton seemed less active than usual, spending hours searching for peridots in the volcanic sand of the beaches. Nonetheless, we were all fascinated by the approachableness of iguanas and finches and the size of the giant tortoises.

The art activities in Virginia City went on as usual that summer, even though Hilton was suffering from angina. Late in August I went to a summer session at Principia College, in Elsah, Illinois, and then on to Sarasota, to get things organized for the winter season in Florida.

Hilton Leech died on October 18th in Montana at age 63, and was buried in the little Virginia City Cemetery. I flew out in late October to drive Dorothy, and dog Folly, home in their station wagon. Some passes in Yellowstone Park were closed due to snow but by going the long way around we got to our usual route out of the mountains. We crossed Togwatee Pass in a snowstorm, something for which my winters in Florida had not prepared me. Dorothy was strong and calm and we got safely to our usual log cabin motel in Dubois, Wyoming, and on to see Jerry at college in Fort Collins, Colorado.

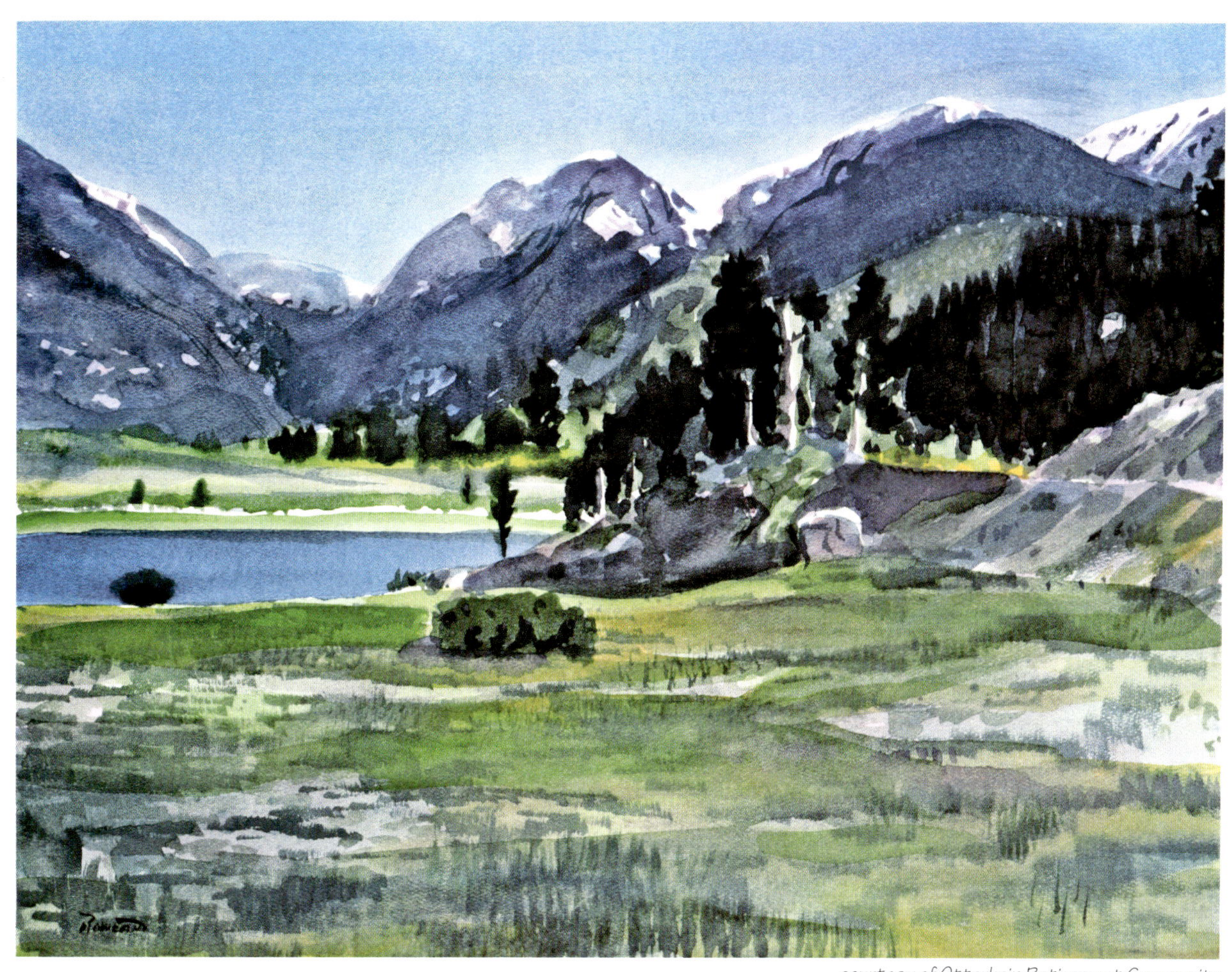

SHEEP MEADOW
oil 1961
42x50

The death of Hilton Leech in the fall of 1969 was a tremendous blow to everyone. Dorothy wanted to keep the school going, both in Sarasota and Montana, and the art communities rallied around to honor Hilton's memory. When the Sarasota brochure had been issued in September 1969, instructors were listed: Hlton Leech, watercolor, and Elden Rowland, oil and experimental. However, before the season opened early in January, 1970, registrations were already being taken for workshops with such well-known artists as William Pachner of Clearwater, and Ben Stahl of Sarasota. Elden's "Intuitive Painting" class was filled to capacity.

Gordon and Emily Holmes were an invaluable source of strength in this challenging time. Emily completed *The Joys of Watercolor ,* which Hilton had been writing at the time of his death. Emily, Dorothy and I became the Workshops Committee. Gordon's financial expertise was priceless. Marc Moon, from Akron, Ohio, was the first out-of-state instructor and Valfred Thelin, from Ogunquit, Maine, soon followed. John Jay Jenkins, who was President of the Friends of the Arts and Sciences, and a close friend of the Leeches, stabilized FAS.

The challenges for me in that winter of 69-70 had just begun. In addition to all of the arrangements for workshops, field trips, exhibitions, etc., I listed over 500 of Hilton's paintings in preparation for appraisal by Frank Oehlschlaeger. When my mother died in February I went to Ohio for the funeral and to see about selling her house. In April, I went with the FAS group on their spring tour to Spain and Portugal and roomed with Dorothy Leech. In late June, while preparing to leave for Montana, a stepladder fell under me as I was pruning a rampant Brazilian pepper and my right shoulder was broken. Nonetheless, I flew to Cleveland to meet Elden and drive with him to Montana where he was to teach that summer. We lived in the little white frame house that the Leeches bought for the Virginia City School. It was called "Buffalo House;" their home was "Eagle." Ray Campeau, a former student, well-known painter and dynamic director of high school art in Bozeman, became the mainstay teacher in Montana.

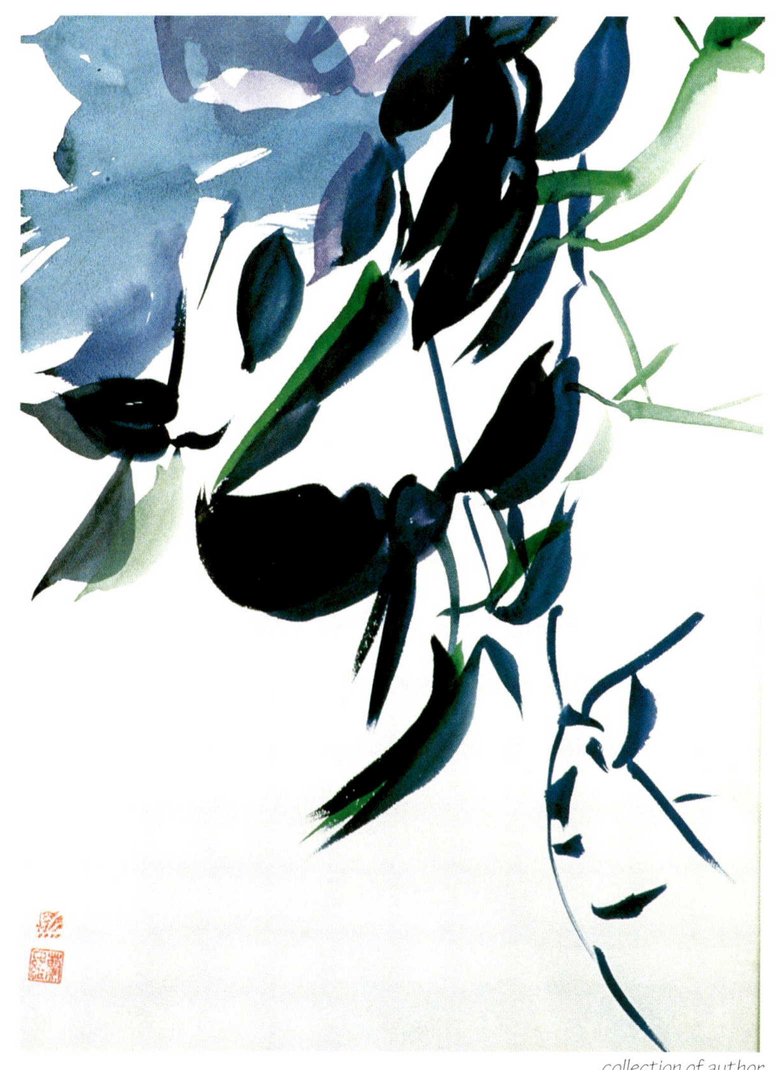

collection of author

SHADOW PATTERNS
watercolor
18x24

In the early 1970s Elden did a series of found-object collages. We spent many happy evenings rambling the hills in Montana looking for crushed metal objects weathered to an appealing texture. The objects were assembled on canvas and the whole finished in warm tones of brown or rust.

 In 1971 "Transition," a 48 x 60 inch found-object collage, won the $500 second purchase prize in the Berkshire Art Association's Annual Regional at Pittsfield, Massachusetts. "It was one of 97 pieces selected by juror John I. H. Baur, director of Whitney Museum, New York, from work submitted by artists from all over New England and New York State.The award ceremony was presided over by Massachusetts Governor Francis W. Sargent," according to an item in the *Sarasota Herald-Tribune.*

In 1971, his found-object work in the Sarasota Art Association's Arvida show, called forth this comment by Charles Benbow, *St, Petersburg Times writer:* "makers of chaotic non-objective abstractions can learn from Elden Rowland's

merit ribbon winner. His triptych canvas, with crushed beer cans and other debris attached, comes close to being ugly (being all in browns) except that the arrangement has rhythm, variety within unity, and the other ingredients that aren't simply a matter of taste but which were proven centuries ago to be necessary for lasting visual interest."

In 1973, "Town House," a six-section cloth collage, was one of four $100 first prizes for paintings at the Cooperstown, New York, 38th National Exhibition. "Sand Painting" had been in the 36th Annual at Cooperstown.

In this period, Elden seemed to be experimenting with different materials as a means of making his own statement. Nonetheless he included the new techniques in his class routines and public demonstrations. In "contact" painting, he spread large areas of color over a sheet of plastic, crumpled it up, and made a contact print from it, using accidents to start a painting. On the other hand, "Red Print," which he called a "dip," seems to be subjective, controlled, maybe intellectual, certainly not accidental.

124

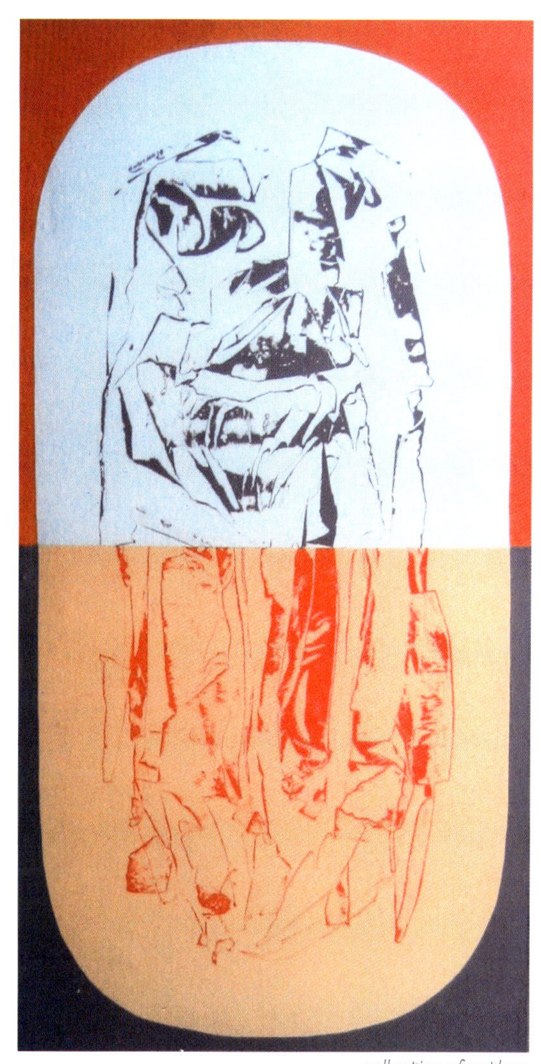
collection of author

RED PRINT
mixed media 1973
20x28

Elden's many styles of painting could give the impression of an indecisive person with fragmented drives. However, there were three factors central to his life as an artist: his interest in all things Oriental, his devotion to his painting career, and his passion for teaching. Part and parcel of the last was his eagerness to be helpful to others. His habit of giving his paintings away may have been a product of all three. "The Bird That Came Home" was given to artist John Barends at a Leech Studio demonstration. Years later, John kindly gave it to me.

Certainly, Elden's self-publishing of his small book *The Painter's Sutra,* was an expression of his desire to help his students express themselves through their painting. In his letter of June 13, 1972, announcing the book, he said, "It presents a synthesis of my teaching, both traditional and contemporary, over the past twenty-five years. . . I have produced a first hand-lettered edition myself, 1,000 numbered copies, especially for students of the 'Intuitive Painting' classes. . . This is not a 'how-to' book, nor a 'personality' book, but a simple modest little book of a philosophical nature. The writing style is modeled on that of the ancient sutras of Buddhism, and the page decorations are intuitively derived from blots. . . I wish I did not have to charge you for it, but I have had to pay for the printing." The charge was $5.

Elden's interest in Oriental things—history, culture, religion, art—went back into his adolescent years. When I met him he was 22, I was 19. He delighted in reciting all the Dynasties of Imperial China, and the years of their reigns. This, along with his being able to read and write almost 1,000 characters of the Japanese language, was very impressive to a young farm girl with a strong Presbyterian background. As the years went on, he read more deeply into Buddhist writings, and I became interested in Christian Science. It might have seemed that this would have caused problems, but it did not. Although I did not try to understand his way of thinking, he did read extensively in Mary Baker Eddy's writings and felt there were great similarities. His Oriental studies strongly affected him, his painting, and his teaching.

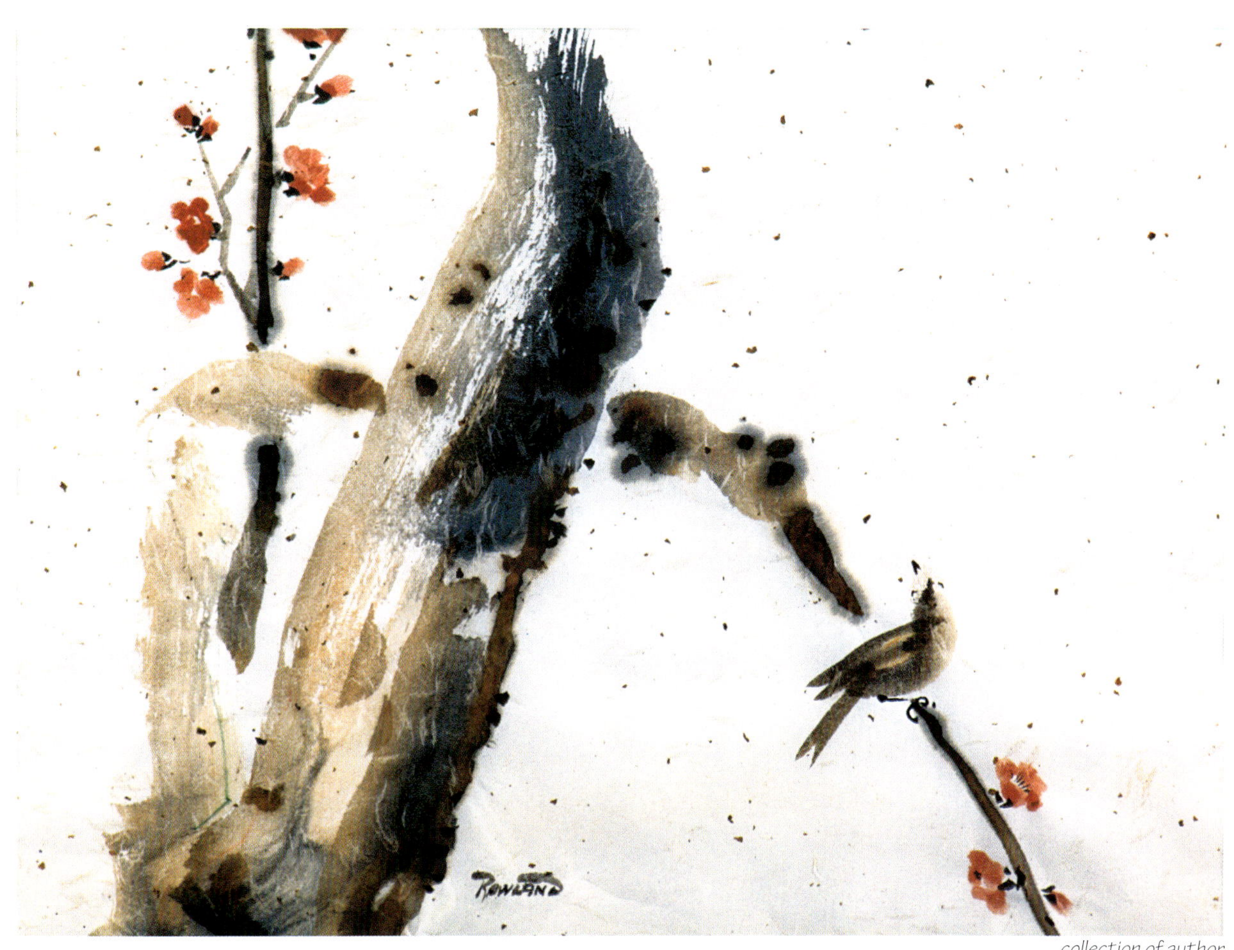

collection of author

BIRD THAT CAME HOME
sumi-e
24x18

Elden did many different Buddha paintings, in many different styles. In "Amitabha Buddha," his oil collage technique gives an impression of an ancient image on a mouldering wall. He had a system of identifying slides of his work by using Japanese characters, presumably efficient for him, but not helpful to a researcher who came later. Titles were confusing to newspapers, too. When Hilton Leech and Elden had a dual show at Stetson University and the Clearwater Art Group, although the painting reproduced well in the local papers, the title was variously reported.

Elden's records gave no explanation about the name "Amitabha" but information in the World Wide Web says: "Amitabha Buddha, the Buddha of Infinite Light and Boundless Life. . . who presides over the Land of Ultimate Bliss . . . and creates this paradise from his compassion to save all living beings. . . "

Elden taught frequent workshops. The summer of 1970, he presented his "Intuitive Painting" classes in Denver, Colorado. The release by the public relations person for the Denver Area Artist Group that sponsored it, said, "In case you don't know what it means either, take the workshop and find out."

He also found time to go on some of the Friends of the Arts and Sciences' trips, including one planned and escorted by Pat Matthews to the Northwest and Alaska. In Seattle, through Pat, we met Robert Sisson, a *National Geographic* photographer whose work I had admired since I first began to receive the magazine in 1940. Robert Sisson and Pat were later married, and he taught at the Leech Studio. The Nature Photography Workshops had started a few years earlier with James H. "Pete" Carmichael. Margarette Mead, Shirley Hummel, and Robert Pelham later joined the staff of teachers.

As time went on, I began to plan and escort all of the FAS trips in the U.S. and Canada. It was a time-consuming responsibility, but it was gratifying to be able to provide educational and enter-taining experiences for so many interested, and interesting, people.

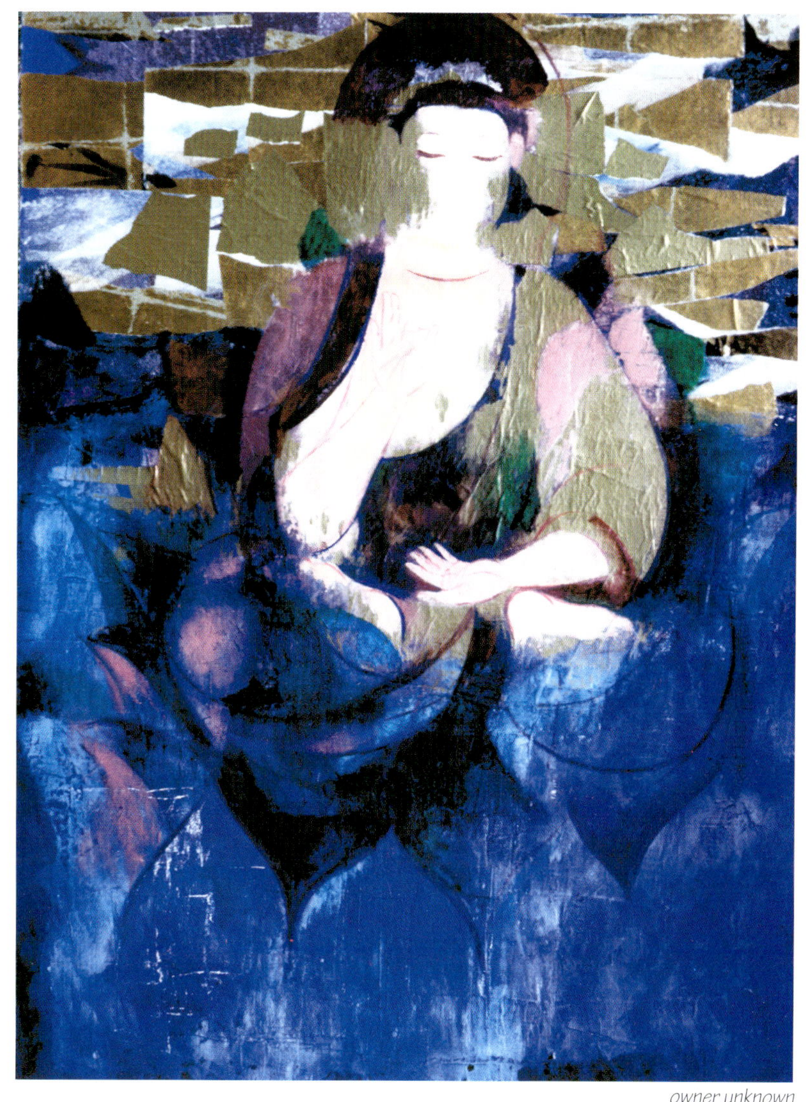

AMITABHA BUDDHA
mixed media 1963

Elden and I put an addition on our home on Siesta Key in the winter of 1971-72, adding almost two-thirds to the square footage of the little house we had built in 1948. Planned by architect Sumner Darling, the addition included a large master bedroom and bath, laundry room, and entry. Sumner and his wife, well-known potter Ann Darling, had become our good friends while Sumner served as president of the Friends of the Arts and Sciences. In spite of being fully-involved at the Leech Studio, I enjoyed acting as "contractor" for the addition, hiring carpenters, ordering materials, etc.

That spring Elden's studio and our house were on the Fine Arts Society's annual tour. "Dryads," a diptych which insinuated female figures into a background of luxuriant foliage in green and gold, was hung on the wall of the new big bedroom, and, except for a one-man show at the Marilyn Bendell Gallery in Cortez, it remained there for many years until it was sold to the Now and Then Gallery of Siesta Key.

The Leech Studio Workshops and Friends of the Arts and Sciences activities flourished during the 1970s. Because of the size of the Studio, membership in FAS had to be limited to 200 and there were long waiting lists. The workshops, too, usually were filled to the capacity of 25. FAS spring and fall tours ranged from South America to Alaska. The list of foreign tours was expanded to include Christmas holiday trips to any place warm, a pattern that had been established by the Leeches and the Matthews and their friends, John D. and Dorothy MacDonald. Elden overcame his reluctance to fly and enjoyed some of the members' trips, including a Caribbean Cruise.

The summer of 1973, I drove Dorothy Leech out to Montana in my new converted-van camper. Flo Schneider, women's editor of *The Journal* wrote about our "summer fun trip in the Blue Beastie" with photos by John Cloud. Flo, with her folksy, but not gossipy, column gave the Friends' activities good support. She, and her sister, Bidie Valade, and friends Eleanor Hodgins and Marlys Fixx—a delightful foursome —participated in many Friends' trips and Studio openings.

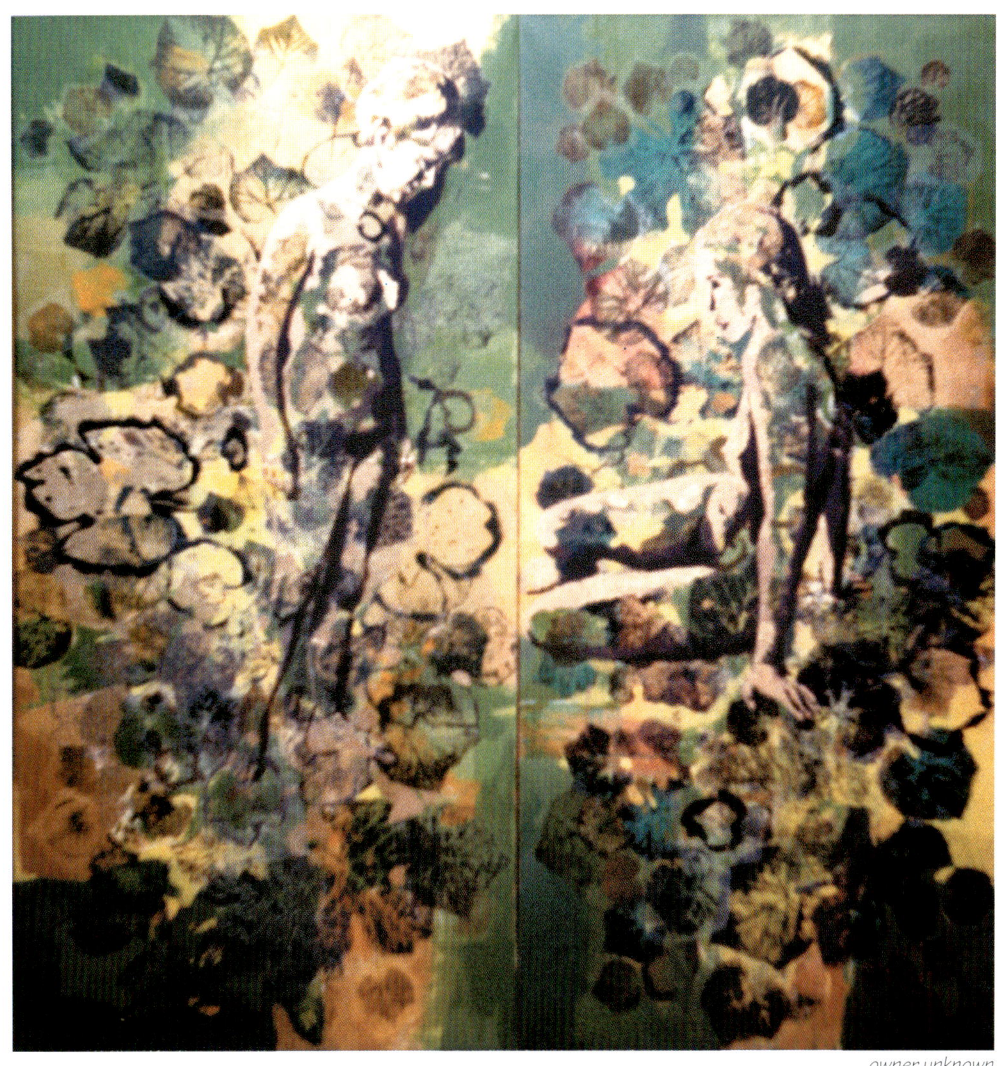

DRYADS
collage 1969
50x40

131

Sumi-e, Intuitive Painting, Oriental Ways with Watercolor, Shadowgraphs, Nature, the Inexhaustible Source—were all names of workshops Elden taught incorporating Oriental techniques and philosophy.

Sumi-e, often called Japanese Ink Brush Painting, was described by Elden in one of his brochures: "Sumi-e is a Japanese term meaning, literally, 'Ink-picture.' Related to Oriental calligraphy, it develops, and requires, great skill in brush control and handling.

"Shadowgraphs are paintings derived from natural shadows, in watercolor or oil, in which the shadows are regarded as an endless source of designs and subjects, or a starting point for paintings either abstract or realistic." The canvas or sheet of water-color paper was placed under shadows, usually of leaves of a tree, and then with quick strokes of color, the pattern was traced in. Advantage was taken of the slight movement that appeared in the patterns as the relative position of the sun changed, the Oriental quality of the work enhanced by the two Rowland signature chops.

Haiku were often used to help the student with the chronic complaint, "I don't know what to paint." The simplicity and clarity of the short ancient Japanese poems served to get student started, or to discourage the over-complication in which a student might be involved. The original 17 syllables, in a 5-7-5 form did not translate exactly into English, but were still beautifully suggestive:

"Far across low mist, intermittently, the lake lifts a snow-white sail."
Or—
 "Dead my old fine hopes, and dry my dreaming, but still—iris, blue each spring."

Elden kept a box filled with things he needed to go out to do a demonstration or workshop: several sizes of round bamboo brushes, a 3-inch flat Hake brush, ink stick and a stone in which to rub it, a box of watercolors, a haiku book, a hand-thrown pot in which to wash his brushes, small sheets of Japanese paper. The materials themselves were works of art. "Iris" was folded up in that box, a sample of Oriental Ways with Watercolor.

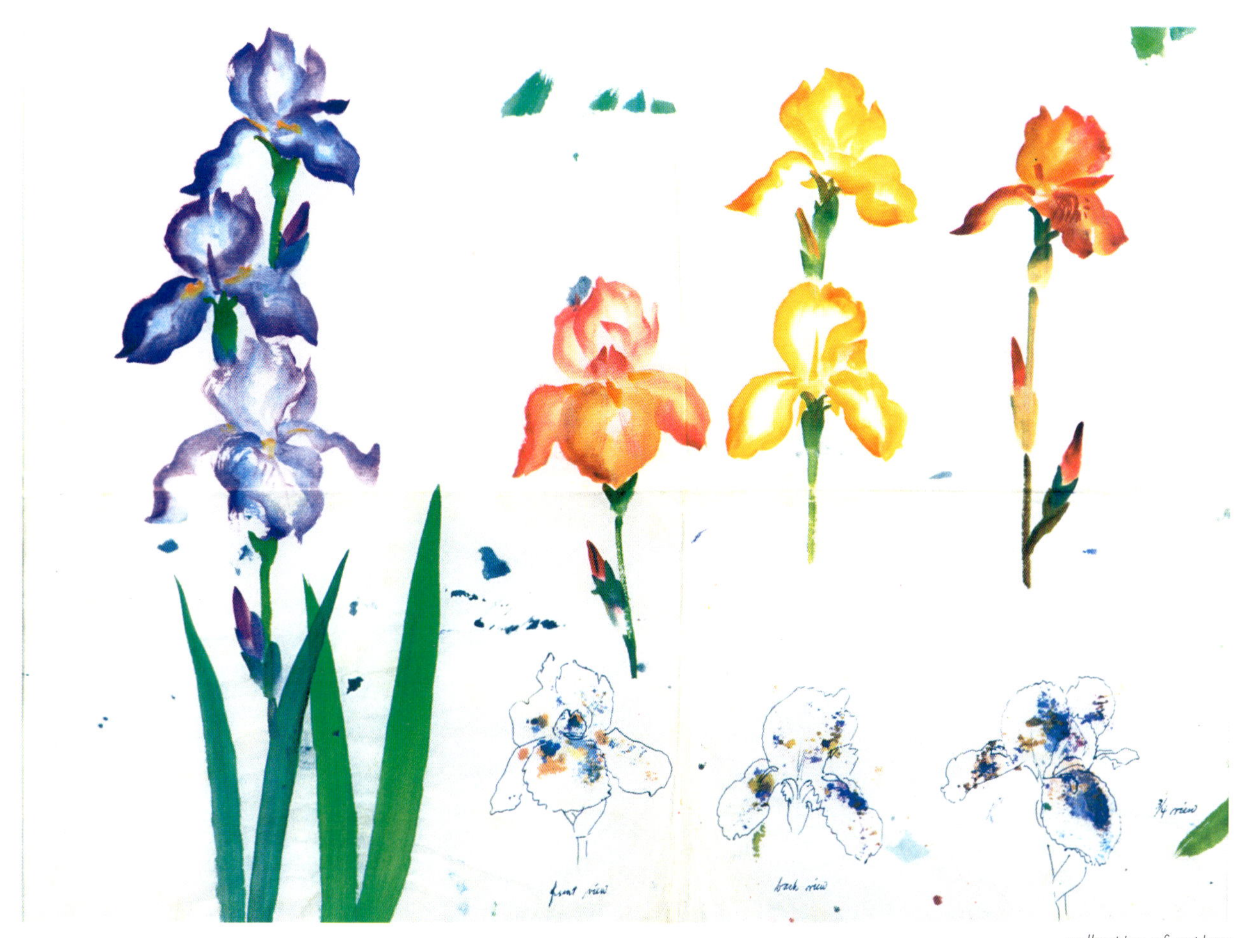

collection of author

IRIS
sumi-e
24x18

Elden's purpose in teaching Oriental ways with watercolor was not to have his students do Oriental paintings, but rather to help them enjoy their learning experiences. In his later years he did many paintings in the traditional Western watercolor techniques.

The Leech Studio remained as a Watercolor Studio, in the tradition in which Hilton Leech had started it. Workshops instructors covered many approaches to watercolor in their classes but no one was teaching watercolor portrait or figure work. We considered having Elden fill in that lack. In looking ahead to the classes, Elden went back to his sketchbooks and painted many watercolor nudes. The classes never were offered; however, it resulted in Elden's amassing a store of delicately-colored, sensitive figure paintings.

Elden's watercolors were shown at the Leech Studio, January 3-22, 1982, together with photographs by Mary Calvert and Agnes Reigart. "Nude Back" was purchased by Emily and Gordon Holmes from that show.

His large Retrospective Exhibition at the Sarasota Art Association in the fall of 1979 had been predominantly oils and mixed media, as were also his works that were circulated by the State Department in their Art in Embassies Program to exotic places such an Ankara, Turkey, and London, England, and San Jose, Costa Rica.

The Friends of the Arts and Sciences' programs and Leech Studio workshops continued to be popular. The 1975, the April bus trip to the Gulf Coast, New Orleans and St. Francisville, was so oversold that it went again in May.

The new Two Arts Traveling Workshops, with painting and photography instructors, were originated in 1978 with Valfred Thelin and Pete Carmichael. Margarette Mead and Alice DeCaprio came later. I planned the trips to allow work periods and we had daily picnic lunches that were great fun. While the others worked, I took the bus and driver and bought the makings for a feast for as many as 40 people. We even had a birthday cake in Yellowstone National Park and ice-cold watermelon at Canyon de Chelly.

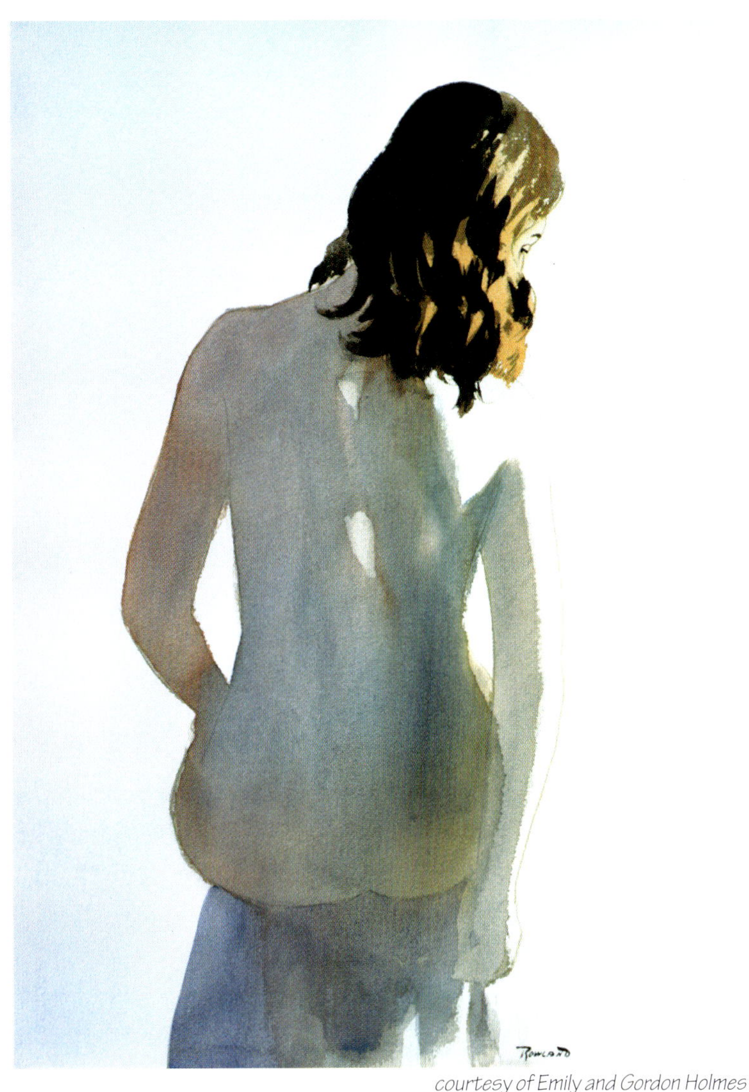

NUDE BACK
watercolor 1980

Elden's health began to deteriorate in the late 1970s. In a summer when he was teaching in New York State, a doctor incompletely removed a melanoma. After that, his energy declined. Two major surgeries resulted in times of remission. Nonetheless, he continued in many activities.

He was president of the Friend of the Arts and Sciences two years. We spent some weeks in Vermont where I was taking a course in lichenology. Another summer we rented a cottage on Penobscot Bay, Deer Isle, Maine.

Elden enjoyed using his 35 mm camera and often sat in on Pete Carmichael's work-shops. In September of 1981 he went with the Two Arts Group to the Northeast and Nova Scotia which included an evening picnic at Val Thelin's house in Ogunquit, Maine. The groups usually gave me a memento as a token of appreciation for my work as coordinator. This time it was a small painting of a buffalo by Val, a great addition to my bison collection which I started when I found an old skull up Williams Gulch in Montana.

In May of 1980, a FAS group went to China, but Elden did not want to go. Called Classical China, it was arranged by Lindblad especially for us. We flew by way of San Francisco and Hong Kong. It was a good time to go before the crowds of tourists began. Our hotels were of old Chinese style, except in Bejing where we stayed in the same Guest House in which President Nixon had stayed on his groundbreaking visit.

I brought brushes and two signature chops home to Elden. I was surprised to find that the Chinese had the characters for such names as "Rowland" and "Katherine." Elden had long ago carved a small soapstone chop, an adaptation of the Rowland family crest, which he used as his logo for his Traveling Exhibition Service. "Ultimate Mountain," reminiscent of the classical shapes painted by the Chinese, was the last demonstration Elden did for the Friends of the Arts and Sciences. Always the showman, he tore the mountain shape in Craft paper, and used his new 5" Chinese Hake brush to make the typical karst mountain shape the group had seen on the Li River, Kweilin, China, appear as if by magic.

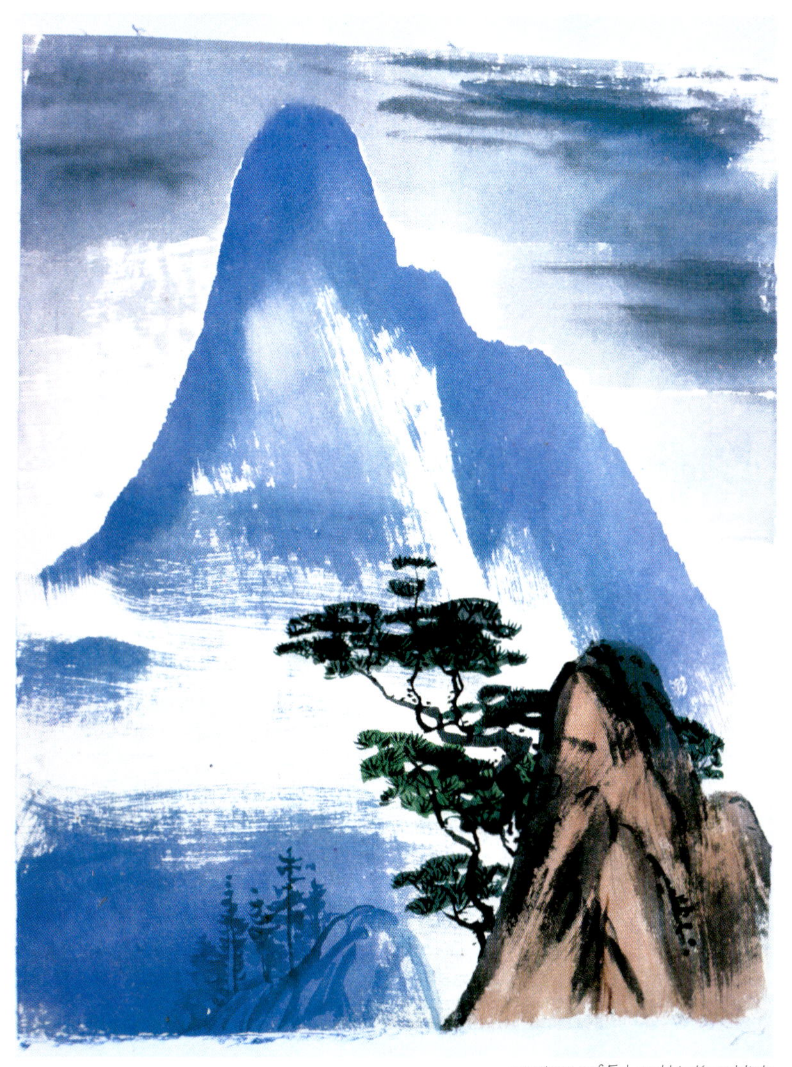

courtesy of Ed and Liz Kornblith

ULTIMATE MOUNTAIN
watercolor 1981
24x40

Elden died on February 22, 1982. He would have been 67 on May 31. At a memorial service in Sarasota, one of the speakers was the Rev. Kevin C. Brown, Chaplain at New College. He had visited Elden several times during his illness and the two had a good rapport because Rev. Brown was also interested in Buddhism. Dr. George Starcher, a distinguished educator whose wife was one of Elden's students, said:

"We salute Elden: a gentle man and a true gentleman, industrious in his habits, public-spirited in his attitudes, charitable in his daily life and associations with others, beloved in his home and admired in his community; a man of candor and courage, intelligence and integrity; a distinguished and boldly affirmative person. Elden was humble, wise, sensitive to the opinions of others, utterly unselfish, deeply committed—not only to a personal faith but also to the deeper purposes and objectives of the work that so completely engaged his energies. . He leaves a wonderful heritage."

A few days before Elden's death, William Hartman, respected artist and teacher at the Ringling School of Art, had written to the Fine Arts Society: "Elden Rowland has served the art community well. No other artist to my knowledge has devoted as much time and effort to promoting the work of his fellow artists. . . His work is an enrichment and a delight."

I designated The Sarasota Art Association as the recipient of gifts in memory of Elden. For a number of years afterward, the Elden Rowland Memorial Award was given in a members' show.

Aware of the havoc that Florida climate and insects could inflict on paper and brushes, I quickly found suitable homes for such things: his small collection of Japanese prints went to the Morikama Museum at Delray Beach; books on Buddhism, to Rev. Brown for New College; and watercolor paper and sable brushes to other artists.

I was fortunate to have a home and a job in which I could go on. That summer, in my camper van, I went all the way to Washington State exploring for four tours.

POEMS BY KATHERINE

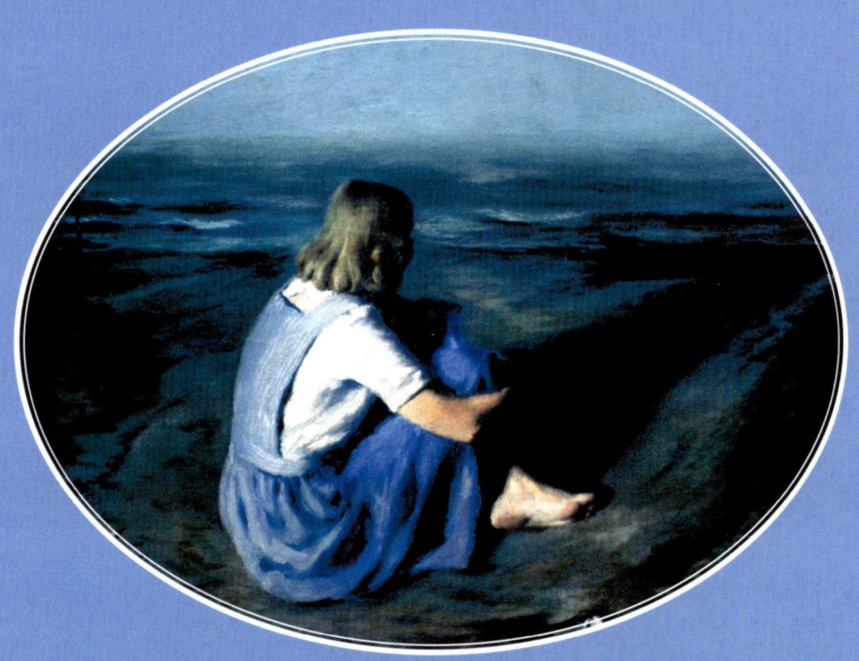

Mr. Howes' Hay Field

In the summer of 1948 my husband and I
Lived in Mr. Howes' hay field high above Cape Cod Bay
Small area in the center of the field—called The Camp
Set aside in frugal, income-producing way

We there for the season, in Covered Wagon house trailer
Top painted blue, bottom gray
Befitting our migratory life between North and South
So husband could paint, I use my secretarial skills

Our neighbors, seeking relief from heat in Boston,
New Bedford, or even New York, coming and going
With wall-sided tents, ropes tugging at deep-seated stakes,
Faded white canvas billowing, flapping in the sea breeze

All around, a riot of color, a tantalizing array of fragrances
Which we called wildflowers, Mr. Howe called hay
White daisies, yellow brown-eyed Susans, red clover, purple vetch
With only a single path cut through, leading down to the beach

Some mornings I, waving good-bye to my husband already at work
In his little balcony attached to Mr. Howes' silver-shingled barn,
Took the path and walked along the rock-strewn shore to type manuscript
For well-known author, struggling to craft a sequel to last year's best seller.

One evening, this writer/friend, wife and four-year old daughter
Graciously accepted our invitation to celebratory dinner in Hyannis
After my husband's first painting sale, thereby providing an indelible memory
Of little girl, firmly, reasonably, insisting on her OWN lobster

The season rolled on, sparkling, sunny days—and nights—Oh, the nights!
Sights—of huge dome sky filled with stars, unbelievably many, unbelievably bright,
Sounds—water lapping on the shore - oft times crashing, then distant fog horn, too
Smells—Bonfire, and bacon, of late-arriving neighbor's hastily prepared supper.

One day, suddenly, Mr Howes appeared, diminutive behind two huge Percherons
Pulling a long-bladed mower, which he guided skillfully, methodically,
All around the field, cutting down our wildflowers—
Just in time to avoid their going to seed, becoming weeds in next year's hay!

The smell of fresh-cut swaths, the sound of Mr. Howes' reedy voice, Gee, Haw, Whoa!
Climaxing memories of that long-gone summer, but most cherished of all,
Still, after all these years, the friendship of that determined little girl
Grown now, into strong, sure, caring womanhood—fulfilling her promise!

—Katherine Lollar Rowland
November 1999

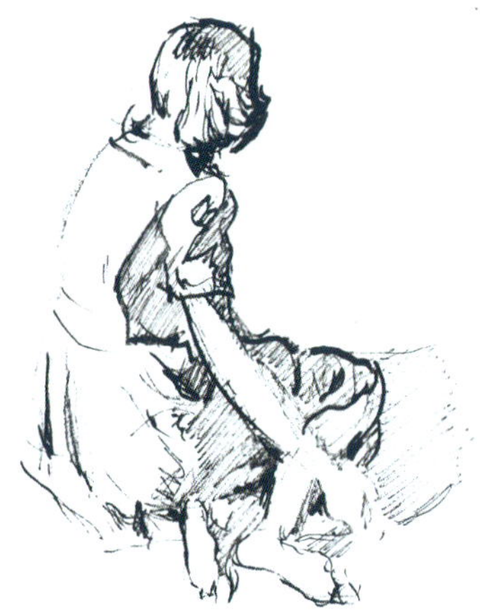

MR. HOWES' BARN

Summer of 1948, art-student husband and I
Live in Mr. Howes' hay field
In East Dennis, high above Cape Cod Bay
Work in silver-shingled barn, he painting, I posing

Spend memorable days on a series of oils called "Girl on the Beach"
Mystery of how earth meets sea
Timeless figure in pinafore gazing pensively at misty infinity
Pieces of flotsam and jetsam seeming surreal in sharply-angled light

As we work on hayloft balcony we pause occasionally
To look out over the water to watch a whale cruising by
To listen to the sea birds cry, to hear laughter of children
Scrambling back as advancing surf, cold and stinging, reaches their toes

Time moves on, paintings completed sell in Hyannisport gallery
Win popular prize in Boston competition
But summer's end leaves unfinished canvases
Rolled and placed in the rafters under the eaves of Mr. Howe's barn

Now all these years later I often think
Of those abandoned canvases
Suspecting, realistically, that they are no longer there
Even—could it be—Mr. Howes' barn and hayfields gone, too?

But no, not gone, here yet—in memories bright and clear
Prompted, as I travel the world, by smell of turpentine, or fresh-mown hay,
Or sight of mysterious light slanting off misty sand and sea—
No matter where, by chance, they happen to come to me

—Katherine Lollar Rowland
November 1999

LOVE AFFAIR

I have a longstanding, never-ending delightful
Love affair with MY COUNTRY
Forty-eight contiguous states, Alaska, Hawaii
Canada, too, East to West

When I was a small child, family of close friends
(Father was out rural mail carrier,
Children all went to one-room school with Brother and me)
Went camping West, tent attached to side of touring car

That was the beginning for me, imagination sparked—
Later, first seeing of mountains, ocean, Washington D.C.
Honeymoon in old Plymouth car
Generously loaned by Ohio farm parents

Then came a lifetime exploring with artist husband
He recording with photo and brush and pen
Storing in memory with well-trained eye
Nature's wonders for future sharing in watercolor and oil

Fifty years as residents on semi-tropical Florida
Meant happy summers in other places called home
Cape Cod, North Carolina Mountains, Montana
And the Midwest, too, in search of my far-reaching roots

I traveled the world—China, the Galapagos, Scotland
But always I came back to MY COUNTRY, my land—
So varied, so accessible by generations of cars
Grateful always for endless new delights, mine, still, to discover, to love

—Katherine Lollar Rowland
Lebanon, Ohio November 11, 1999

Images of Best Friend

Growing up on a farm in the Midwest I went to a one-room school
The only other girls my age lived down the graveled road
Almost two miles away; shy, too soon tall, too dignified, they said,
I longed for a Best Friend

Things changed, as things do, happily married
Artist husband and I went to spend summers on Cape Cod
And there I found a Best Friend
The opposite of me

Infectious laugh, positive attitude, quickly moving to see what's next
Rounded, short, freckles, carrot-top hair,
Befitting her Scottish heritage
A teacher in Boston during the school year, she spent summers free

With her father, crony of the oystermen, gathering harborside
Swapping stories, at Mr. Higgins' Spit and Chatter Club
Sprawling silver-shingled shed, on pilings
Listing dangerously above the spectacular rise and fall of the tide

First art student of my husband, she, in her outgoing way, persuaded me
To leave imagined duties in our peripatetic home among the pines
To experience, enjoy, such a captivating, unique place, as
Cape Cod, before National Seashore popularity

We had such good times, my Best Friend, my husband and I
While he worked enthusiastically at his painting, teaching, gallery sitting
She and I explored shifting dunes and tawny marshes almost
To historic Land's End, down Provincetown way

Walking the back roads, traces, really, from times long past
We found rank, scraggly lilac bushes, sure sign that early settlers had been there
And empty cellar holes, tantalizing evidence of unrecorded dreams and lives,
All the while, talking, sharing, she introducing me to her faith, a joyful way of life

Broken black lines on Coast and Geodetic Survey map
Led us to abandoned settlements
Indian Neck and Bound Brook Island;
Confirming stories told to us by true Cape Codders,

Long descended in this place,
About where ship wrecks might still be found
Beneath the crashing surf on the Ocean Side,
Just below High Land Light

On sunny days, Best Friend, my husband and I—even our Siamese cat, picnicked
Among the waving grasses high above the beach
Devouring lobster, and fresh peas, and blueberries, provender just that morning
Sought out from favorite small scale entrepreneurs in the community

In the evening, warmth and camaraderie in much-photographed apple pie cottages
In the Village Center on Gardner's Hill; how can I forget
Laughing hilariously when she as a special treat for her teacher, baked a blueberry pie
And, tripping on the topmost step, deposited it triumphantly at his feet?

Later, she invited me to come to the mainland to be with her when her father died.
Her family looking quite askance, she and I went to downtown movie house
To see "Fantasia", just released by Disney, an indication of her buoyant spirit,
A celebration of her father's life

Later still, she came to spend mid-winter holiday with us on Florida's West Coast
Sharply-etched image of her there on Christmas Day, elbows on abandoned sea wall on
Longboat Key, eating stone crab claws, our special treat for her; seagulls diving,
Screaming, discordant aerial ballet, background bright blue sky, dazzling pure white sand

Though our paths diverged, we never lost touch
She married late in life, my husband's career, our lives,
Took us West, and many places in the world
But still to this very hour come to me, bright, clear, images of one who was my best
Best Friend

—*Katherine Lollar Rowland • Vancouver, Washington • December 19, 1999*

Smokey, the Cat

Recently I sent to my friend Patty, a photograph—
A photograph of Smokey, the Cat
Taken over half a century ago at a picnic
In the dune grass high above a Cape Cod beach

In reply, Patty asked a question of me
"How did the cat react to such a big expanse of freedom?"
What a GREAT question!
Even after a diligent search of my memory bank, I have not even a hint

The photograph shows Smokey, the Cat
In typical Siamese pose, stalking some imaginary prey
Free indeed, free of the red leather harness we had for him
To which was sometimes attached a long read leather leash

The harness and leash come to us with him
Through the open door of blacksmith shop turned art studio
In the oysterman's village where we spent the summer—
His previous owner, a man who worked in the city, New York

There he had lived a solitary cat life, with only occasional walks in Central Park
We didn't even know his name, so he became Smokey, the Cat
Full time companion for my husband and me
At first, neurotic, telling us all about it in full-blown Siamese voice

Later, as we became attuned, he liked to walk with us, explore,
When we went some place free of people and dogs—
Dogs, large and small, were a challenge to him
He loved to scratch them on the nose

I cannot reconstruct that particular picnic on that long-ago sunlit day
I cannot recall any problem getting him from car

To hidden spot in the high beach grass
He must have followed after us, in his usual way

Head held high, velvety brown ears alert, nose twitching, sniffing the air,
Eager to meet, and greet, any possible admirers—
Or was it just to detect any left-over bits of lobster
From someone else's feast?

All of which brings me to conjecture, as I often have before
About the relationship of memory, and photographs, and family lore
We had so many treasured stories about Smokey, the Cat
Who liked to walk with us, and talk to us, and travel with us (unless it was hot)

How much of what we store in our memory bank
Is real, or only our perception of the real
Filtered through layer on layer of experiences over the years,
Sharpened, sometimes, by photographs, like this one of Smokey, the Cat?

Without it, and many others of its ilk,
Would memory of him, and happy times we shared, grow dim?
I think not, though sadly, others who were there, then,
Are not here, now, to look back, and reminisce with me

—Katherine Lollar Rowland
Siesta Key, Sarasota
January 24, 2000

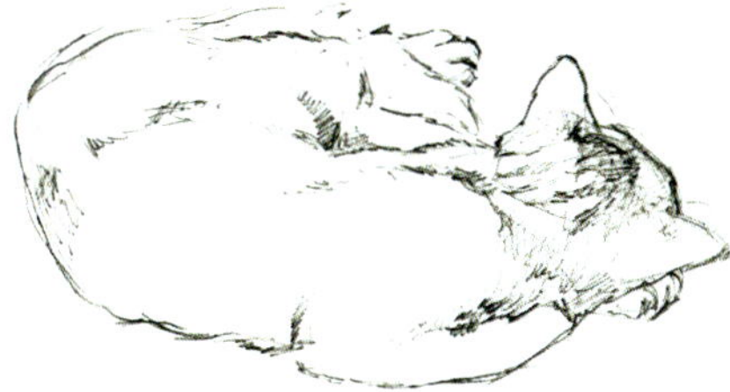

WALK ON THE BEACH

I've been away from the Siesta Key
My home for fifty years -
Now I've come back,
At least, temporarily

Early evening today, I walk down to the beach
Just three blocks away, public pavilion now, but quite deserted
When we brought our piece of Florida, built our dream house, so many years ago
Almost no one else around, it was "our" place to sun and swim

Now, as then, sand, snow-white, sugar fine,
Weaving it's magic spell, enticing me to wander along firm, damp, edge
Crash of advancing surf followed by whisper
Of tumbling bits of shell as it retreats again

Flocks of little shore birds moving in amusing unison
Tiny, graceful automatons, taking to the air as I approach,
Landing again almost immediately to pursue their
Busy search for interesting minute things brought in by every wave

Over the water, not from me, a pelican dives repeatedly, efficiently,
Although to my eyes, awkwardly, for this share of the sea's abundance
Mimicking closely his every move, a smaller bird—
A seagull—I wish I knew why!

The light is changing now as the sun moves lower in the sky
Giving a pink glow to everything, sharply etching ripples in the sand row on row
Tracks, too, of birds, large and small, and joggers, and dogs, I adding something new
Impressions of the tip of walking stick, like benign little antlion traps, conical, ephemeral

Away from water's edge where the sea oats grow, a cluster of small boats,
Light turquoise and white, masts titling, sails furled
Waiting for a sunlit day to be launched on shining blue water,
To go skimming before the breeze

Banks of billowing clouds edged in shining light, backlit
As the sun continues the nightly ritual
Of disappearing over the horizon in the west
Sending spectacular rays into the sky, day's end on Siesta Key

I continue my walk, return to my home, grateful in my heart
For Nature's largess in proving us such a wide, wide beach
Such a beautiful meeting of land and sea, still here in spite of
Traffic rushing back and forth, tall buildings crowding in, menacingly

—Katherine Lollar Rowland
Vancouver, Washington
December 19, 1999

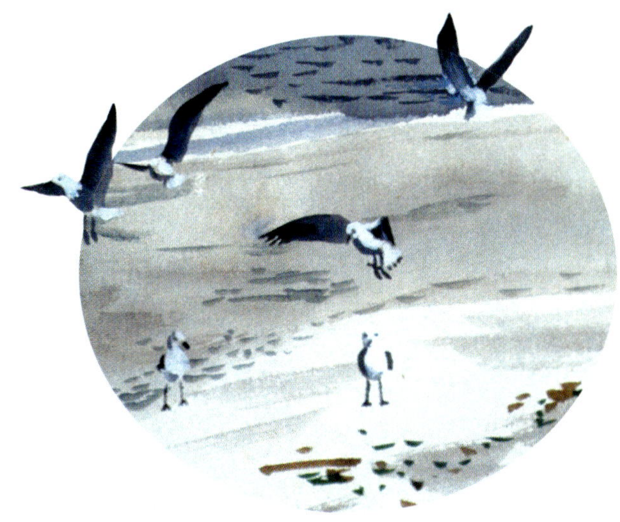

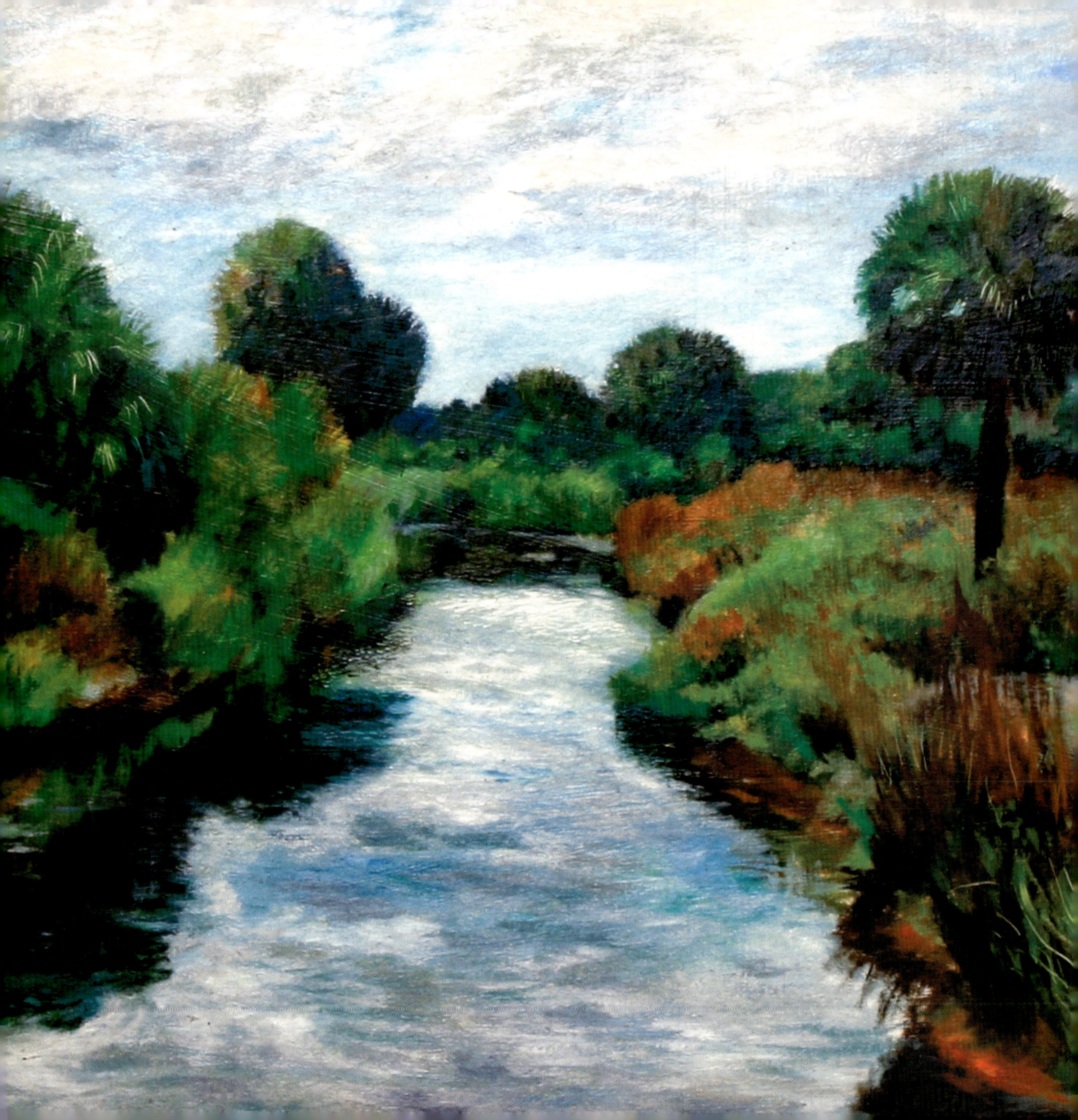

WITH GRATITUDE
TO ALL WHO HELPED

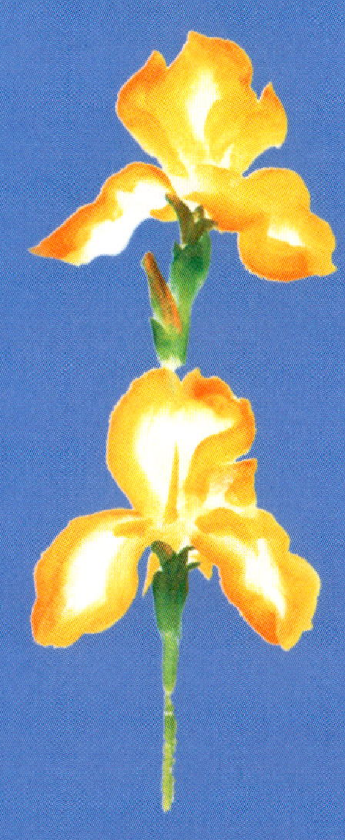

THOSE WHO OWN ELDEN'S PAINTINGS
THAT ARE REPRODUCED:

F. R. Clark

Kathy Lollar and Don Divens

Hushi Garfield

Patty Hodgins

Emily and Gordon Holmes

Liz and Ed Kornblith

Michael Lagerman

Emily Lowe Art Gallery, Miami, Florida

Amy and Eric Magel

Monsanto

Nancy and Dave Myerholtz

Susan Orr

Otterbein-Lebanon Retirement Community, Ohio

Richmond Art Museum, Indiana

Brian Schwarz

Hongfei (Jessica) and Kevin Schwarz

Paula Wilson

THOSE WHO MADE PHOTOTGRAPHS:

Barbour's Photography

Robert Flischel

Tony Grant

Margarette Mead

Ric Miracle

Kevin Schwarz

Joseph Janney Steinmetz

THOSE WHO, AMONG MANY OTHERS, WERE
INTERESTED AND ENCOURAGED:

Patty Hodgins

Jayre Leech

Nancy Leech Daland

Ruth Stevens

Pat Ringling Buck

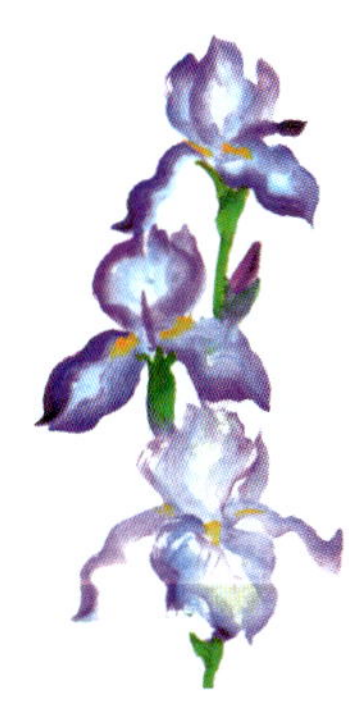

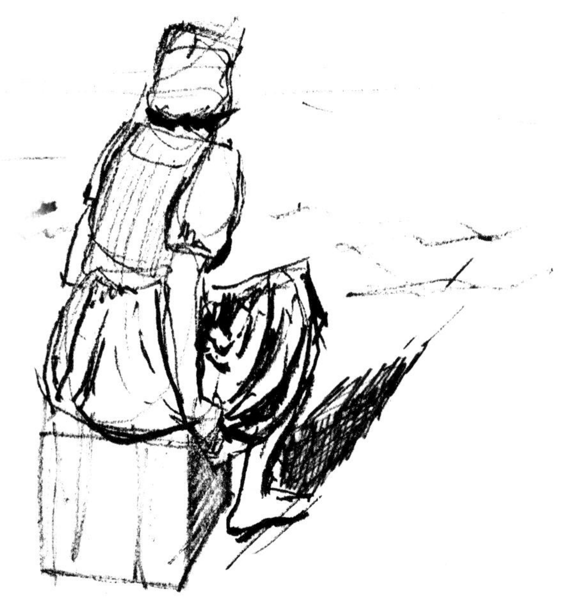